*This book is dedicated
to the courage, resilience and irrepressible hope
of the refugee youth who dared to share their stories,
and dream of peace.*

*100% of the royalties from the sale of this book
will be donated to peacebuilding efforts in Burma.*

PRAISE FOR
FORCED TO FLEE: VISUAL STORIES BY REFUGEE YOUTH FROM BURMA

"Words cannot adequately depict the horrors, fear and grief experienced by refugees, political prisoners and exiles from Burma (Myanmar). In *Forced to Flee*, refugee youth armed with watercolor pencils and drawing paper are able to overcome the limitations of language. If their yellow is a little too bright, and their black a bit too dark, it's a perfect reflection of the larger-than-life incidents that shaped their reality."
—*Kenneth Wong, writer and illustrator*

"*Forced to Flee* manages to interweave the rich tapestry of Burma's ethnic and religious diversity together with the story of Burma's struggle for democracy and human rights through words and pictures that tell human stories of fear, pain, tragedy as well as inspirational courage and hope."
—*Benedict Rogers, author of* Burma: A Nation at the Crossroads

"*Forced to Flee* gives me chills and thrills. Chills for the resistance of human beings against immense violence and injustice under an oppressive culture; thrills for their resilience and continued aspirations for peace and justice … Thank you for inviting these incredible youth to shed light on their stories and dreams."
—*Khin Ohmar, Coordinator, Burma Partnership*

"I sat down to read *Forced to Flee*, and my heart changed … Erika Berg leads the reader on a journey through the book, but also a journey through Burma. Along the way we meet people with stories that will stir your heart. When I was done reading the book, I felt as if I had been running a marathon. The emotions it stirred in me led me up on mountaintops and down to the deepest, darkest valleys."
—*Oddny Gumaer, Founder, Partners Relief & Development*

"*Forced to Flee* brings out the true emotions of those who long for peace, love and freedom as well as the pain and atrocities they have had to go through. It is indeed a powerful book as each picture depicts a touching story that serves as an eye opener for those who do not know about the lives of the refugees, while it will deepen the lasting impression it has made on those who already do."
—*Dr. Alana Golmei, Director, Burma Centre Delhi*

"The visual stories in *Forced to Flee* remind us that faith and dignity can transcend all forms of oppression and deprivation. From extraordinarily diverse ethnic and religious backgrounds, a common sense of identity and a desire for a better future shine through. Reconciliation is possible. And refugees have a very important role to play."   —*Jack Dunford, Executive Director, The Border Consortium, 1984-2012*

"*Forced to Flee* illustrates that the ethnic people of Burma have been detained, abused and forcibly displaced by the Burma Army not because of anything they have or haven't done but because of their native ethnicity and their resource-rich native land. Only when their ethnic diversity is embraced and they are granted equal rights under the constitution will sustainable peace be possible."
—*Khon Ja, Coordinator, Kachin Peace Network*

"*Forced to Flee* illustrates the incredible resilience of Burma's ethnic youth in the face of horrific human rights abuses … The country's leaders could learn so much from the visionary solutions so eloquently expressed here by the youth. They provide such hope for Burma's future."
—*Rachel Fleming, Advocacy Director, Chin Human Rights Organization*

"This long-awaited collection of watercolor paintings by refugee youth, informative captions, behind-the-scenes photographs and contextual material is profoundly moving … *Forced to Flee* exudes sacred wisdom, beauty and hope. I remain deeply touched and inspired."
—*Imam Jamal Rahman, speaker on Islam and interfaith relations*

"Visual storytelling is a powerful window into the complex range of issues and emotions that embody Myanmar's current transition. This book is riveting for those who know the country, and those yet to be captivated by it. The pictures speak many thousands of words."
—*Aela Callan, filmmaker and journalist*

"I was moved to tears by this beautiful and profound book! It is a must-read for those working in the field of migration or mental health. With first-person insights and experiences, it reminds us of what is lost and what remains for those forced to flee."   —*Beth Farmer, Director, Northwest Health and Human Rights*

"*Forced to Flee* was inspired by the stories of youth who have fled persecution in different corners of Myanmar. By documenting their struggles and aspirations with art materials, these brave survivors of injustice challenge Myanmar's leadership to end impunity and promote human rights, including in remote ethnic areas."   —*Wai Wai Nu, Director, Women Peace Network Arakan*

"In *Forced to Flee*, refugee youths' real-life stories illustrate complex issues related to ethnic conflicts, religious tension and political persecution in Burma. The book doesn't just describe the issues; it promotes the voice of refugees who have lived in exile for decades while remaining committed to bringing freedom and peace to their displaced communities."

—*Hayso Thako, Principal, Shalom Arts and Leadership College, Mae La (refugee camp)*

"*Forced to Flee* reflects the real Shan people's life in Shan State and along the Thai-Burma border. I think people who live in cities throughout Shan State should read this book. Then they would understand that in the more remote rural areas of Shan State people continue to suffer from human rights abuses and can only dream of peace."

—*Larn Tai, Shan Youth Power*

"This book is a testament to the indomitable spirit of those who have been forced to flee injustice in Burma, and to the transformative power of art … By highlighting the stories of those who—despite democratic reforms—continue to struggle and suffer in the shadows, the book promises to mobilize greater support for human rights throughout Burma."

—*Tun Khin, President, Burmese Rohingya Organization UK*

"For many years, Erika Berg has worked diligently to open communications between traumatized refugees and the seemingly indifferent communities where they have sought refuge. *Forced to Flee* portrays and honors a genuine, heart-to-heart collaboration."

—*Larry Dohrs, Chairman, U.S. Campaign for Burma*

"The world has been bedazzled by Burma's opening. This dominant narrative often obscures the stories of persecuted peoples whose plight continues … *Forced to Flee* highlights their stories, reminding the world of their plight and that, in many ways, Burma's reforms have truly yet to begin."

—*Dr. Voravit Suwanvanichkij, Johns Hopkins Bloomberg School of Public Health*

"*Forced to Flee* will help readers understand the living situation of the more than 125,000 refugees still living along the Thai-Burma border who were forced to flee their homeland and now are growing up in overcrowded camps without enough nutritious food, health care or education. This book captures their struggles, portrayed by refugee youth who experience them daily."

—*Naw K'nyaw Paw, Secretary, Karen Women's Organization, Burma*

"Human suffering is all too pervasive throughout our world, and it does not diminish when we look away. *Forced to Flee* reminds us that it is the duty of all of us—regardless of who or where we happen to be—to enhance the well-being of the most vulnerable among us and address the roots of their suffering."

—*Garrett Kostin, Director, Burma Study Center*

For resources related to this book, please visit: www.burmavisionsforpeace.org

Copyright © 2015 by Erika Berg

Cover and book design by Alexandra Rösch

Copyediting by Stephanie Lawyer and Garrett Kostin

Photographs by Daniel Kranzler and Erika Berg

Maps by Ta Say and Erika Berg

All rights reserved. No part of this book may be reproduced, stored in a retrieval system or transmitted, in any form or by any means, without the prior written permission of the author.

Print and color management by iocolor, LLP Seattle

Printed in China

ISBN: 978-0-9908910-0-0

FORCED TO FLEE

Visual Stories by Refugee Youth from Burma

Erika Berg

FORCED TO FLEE: VISUAL STORIES BY REFUGEE YOUTH FROM BURMA

CONTENTS

DEAR READER 2

FORCED TO FLEE 4

JOURNEY TO SAFETY 38

LIVING IN EXILE 66

MEMORY 98

HOPES & DREAMS 120

EPILOGUE: BRIDGING DIVIDES 152

WAYS TO HELP 174
THE WORKSHOPS 178
ACKNOWLEDGEMENTS 180
A PERSONAL NOTE 183

Dear Reader,

No one has taught, humbled or inspired me more than refugees. I am in perpetual awe of those who have survived traumatic experiences, devastating losses and heartache yet, somehow, manage to remain determined, hopeful–even grateful.

The visual stories in this book bear witness to the memories, struggles and dreams of young people forced to flee violent conflict and persecution in Burma, also known as Myanmar. They illustrate that emotions conveyed and evoked by a single narrative image can tell a story of a thousand words, open hearts and build bridges of understanding.

Forced to Flee *honors the life stories of youth for whom displacement, loss, exile and uncertainty are ways of life. In the 40 plus visual storytelling workshops that I, with the help of my husband Daniel and young daughter Seki, facilitated along the borders of Burma and in the United States and Canada, refugee youth painted their answers to the following questions:*

Why were you forced to flee Burma?
What do you remember most about your journey to safety?
What is/was it like to live in exile (a refugee camp)?
What do you miss most about Burma?
What is your dream for the future?

Initially, youth questioned why anyone would care about their lives. However, the more deeply they reflected on their experiences and invested in the creative process, the more their confidence grew. Over the course of each workshop, the youth came to realize that genuine reconciliation in a war-torn society depends upon uncovering the truth, however painful. As you will see throughout this book, the youths' stories do matter. By giving voice to their oppressed and marginalized ethnic communities, they promote a more just and inclusive peace in Burma.

Forced to Flee *offers a child's-eye view of the longest-running civil war in the world. Drawn into the youths' inner worlds, you will receive clues as to what it's like to be forced to flee one's homeland and live in exile, haunted–and empowered–by traumas of the past. At the same time, your attention will be called to injustices that continue to be committed throughout the country. Clearly, despite recent democratic reforms, Burma still has a long way to go.*

*If you are moved by the youths' stories, may the "Bridging Divides" epilogue and "Ways to Help" appendix at the end of this book help transform your empathy into inspired action. To learn more and share your reactions to the youths' visual stories, please visit **www.burmavisionsforpeace.org**.*

In gratitude,

Erika Berg
Erika Berg
Seattle, Washington USA

"WHY WERE YOU FORCED TO FLEE BURMA?"

THERE ARE AS MANY REASONS for fleeing one's native land as there are individuals who have fled. Their uniquely individual reasons can be categorized as follows:

REFUGEES flee their country of nationality due to a well-founded fear of ethnic, religious and/or political persecution. Undocumented **MIGRANTS** work or attend school in neighboring countries; often, they too have been forced to flee their country of origin. **INTERNALLY DISPLACED PERSONS (IDPs)** also are forced to flee their villages or communities; however, they continue to live within their country's boundaries. **STATELESS PEOPLE** are not recognized as citizens by any state.

A LARGE PERCENTAGE OF REFUGEES FROM BURMA FLED AS CHILDREN. They survived the violent destruction of their communities, including family and friends. The youth who painted the "visual stories" in this chapter were primarily refugees. However, you also will bear witness to life stories about and by migrant, internally displaced and stateless youth from Burma.

> A **REFUGEE** is someone who has fled his or her country "owing to a well-founded fear of being persecuted for reasons of race, religion, nationality, membership of a particular social group or political opinion, is outside the country of his/her nationality and is unable, or owing to such fear, is unwilling to avail himself/herself of the protection of that country."
>
> —1951 United Nations Convention Relating to the **Status of Refugees**

WHILE COMPRISING AT LEAST 30% OF BURMA'S POPULATION, ETHNIC MINORITIES REPRESENT THE VAST MAJORITY OF VICTIMS OF VIOLENT CONFLICT IN BURMA. The longest-running and deadliest conflicts between the Burma Army and ethnic armies have occurred in ethnic areas, including Arakan, Chin, Kachin, Karen, Karenni, Mon and Shan states, so most of the visual stories in the book were painted by ethnic youth.

Ta Say (23), Kent, Washington, United States

FROM 1962 TO 2011, BURMA WAS RULED BY A SERIES OF OPPRESSIVE AND BRUTAL MILITARY REGIMES. Following a flawed election in 2010, the military government ceded power in 2011 to a quasi-civilian government. However, Burma's constitution dates back to 2008. Drafted by the military junta, the constitution is inherently undemocratic; it reflects and protects the best interests of the military rather than the best interests of the people.

Note: A few of the visual stories in this book were painted by adult hosts and translators of our visual storytelling workshops and by former political prisoners who were also forced to flee. Thanks to their willingness to share their life stories, historical events that youth were not alive to experience first-hand are brought to life.

FORCED TO FLEE

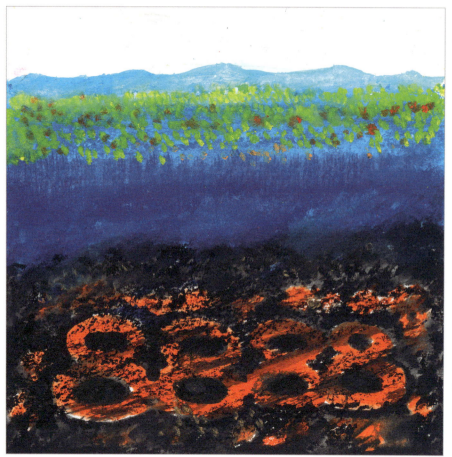

Khaing Htoon (former political prisoner), Mandalay, Burma

The largest national uprising in Burma calling for freedom and democracy erupted on 8 August 1988. Hundreds of thousands of people flooded the streets, demanding an end to the military's repressive rule. Instead, the military gunned down some 3,000 peaceful demonstrators, mostly students. Khaing Htoon was among the students who sacrificed their own personal freedom for the movement. He believed that until the government apologized to survivors of the 8888 Uprising—former political prisoners, their families and everyone else who suffered from the injustices of the former military regime—this open wound would continue to fester and cast doubt on the government's democratic reforms.

"Nothing is going to stop us from

On 8 August 1988, before the military opened fire on demonstrators, a large crowd gathered outside the US Embassy in Rangoon to listen to student democracy activist Min Ko Naing speak: "We, the people of Burma, have had to live without human dignity for 26 years under oppressive rule. We must end dictatorial rule in our country. Only people power can bring down our repressive rulers . . . If we want to enjoy the same rights as people in other countries, we have to be disciplined, united and brave enough to stand up to dictators. Let's express our sufferings and demands. Nothing is going to stop us from achieving peace and justice in our country." San Nyein Oo agreed with Min Ko Naing, who quickly emerged as one of Burma's most tireless and courageous democracy leaders.

San Nyein Oo (former political prisoner), Mandalay, Burma

achieving peace and justice in our country."

FORCED TO FLEE

Thet Naing Oo (former political prisoner), Mandalay, Burma

The military regime's deadly crackdown on the 8888 Uprising cast a shadow over the entire nation. Thousands of activists were arrested. No one felt safe. Yet out of respect for the peaceful protestors who had been massacred, Thet Naing Oo and thousands of other survivors vowed to continue to struggle non-violently against the military's rule and for human rights and democracy, regardless of personal loss. On 26 August, Aung San Suu Kyi—daughter of Aung San, founder of the Burma Army—entered the political arena, calling for the democratization of Burma. Less than a year later, she was placed under house arrest.

Thousands of former political prisoners bear scars of being tortured, physically and psychologically. Some were locked in cramped cells and spent years in solitary confinement. Wrists tied, they were hung from the ceiling of interrogation centers and beaten unconscious. They were forced to stand indefinitely on their tiptoes with nails piercing their soles. Despite their courage and sacrifices, the vast majority of political prisoners remain faceless and nameless to all but the family and friends who have dared to stand by them. Jacob painted this picture to honor Burma's unsung heroes. "Without Burma's political prisoners there would be no democracy movement."

Jacob Lalmuanpuia (16), Aizawl, Mizoram State, India

"Without Burma's political prisoners there would be no democracy movement."

FORCED TO FLEE

Phone Myint, Mae Sot, Thailand

"They just started shooting …" After a long pause, Phone Myint added, "Sometimes I wish I hadn't escaped." When the soldiers couldn't find him, they shot and killed two of his friends. Afraid that Burma's Military Intelligence would find him in the Thai border town of Mae Sot, home to about 200,000 refugees and migrants from Burma, Phone Myint went into hiding. It had been two years since he had last seen his family. He was afraid to tell his wife that he was still alive. He was afraid that he would endanger her and his young son and daughter.

"Sometimes I wish I hadn't escaped."

Ta Say (20), Kent, Washington, United States

Burma has the second largest active army in Southeast Asia. Most soldiers "recruited" into the Burma Army are from poor families, uneducated and especially vulnerable to being brainwashed by military propaganda. Faced with dissent, they have been programmed to choose force over justice. That's how Ta Say remembered the army restoring "harmony"—at gunpoint.

FORCED TO FLEE

Sawmi (35), Aizawl, Mizoram State, India

Students have always been at the forefront of pro-democracy movements in Burma. In reaction to the 8888 Uprising, the government shut down universities—hubs of academic freedom and activism— and didn't reopen them until 1990. A few months later, universities were shut down again after students demanded the release of pro-democracy leader Aung San Suu Kyi. While under house arrest, she had been awarded the Nobel Peace Prize for her non-violent struggle for human rights and democracy in Burma. Another student strike in 1996 led to three more years of closures. When some universities reopened in 1999, the focus shifted to discipline and rote memorization. Students attended classes under close surveillance by Military Intelligence, after agreeing in writing that they would not participate in political activities. "What could be more short-sighted than denying students an education?" Sawmi said, shaking her head.

Before Burma's censorship office closed in 2013 human rights activists using satire to poke fun at the military regime or to portray socio-economic problems in the country risked more than censorship. A former political cartoonist, Nay Myo Aye was arrested and imprisoned for daring to "speak" the truth to power. After being released from prison, he fled to Thailand. As vice principal of a school for migrant youth from Burma, he stressed the importance of standing up for one's beliefs.

Nay Myo Aye (former political prisoner), Mae Sot, Thailand

"*What could be more short-sighted than denying students an education?*"

FORCED TO FLEE

Burma Army battalions have burned down thousands of villages, mostly in ethnic regions of eastern Burma. Ethnic Karen, Saw Yar Zar wasn't the only workshop participant in Mae Sot who had been forced to flee more than one burning village. "I will never forget the smell and crackling sound."

Saw Yar Zar (16), Mae Sot, Thailand

"I will never forget

Naw Hkee Paw (16), Mae Sot, Thailand

Naw Hkee Paw's head tilted forward. Staring glassy-eyed into her painting, she slowly traced with her index finger the distant mountain ridge. As if lost in a haze of memory, she whispered, "We never looked back." At the time, she was a young girl. She didn't know that villagers living near a mine, pipeline, hydroelectric dam or some other government development project were at the greatest risk of violence and forced displacement.

the smell and crackling sound."

FORCED TO FLEE

Luke (23), Vancouver, British Columbia, Canada

Luke's entire village was burned down by the Burma Army. Luke was among more than 500 Karen villagers, suddenly homeless and terrified, left to fend for themselves. Luke's family fled across the Thai-Burma border and, for years, lived in a refugee camp. Looking back, Luke viewed the Burma Army as thieves in a lawless land, free to steal villagers' land, possessions, livelihood and futures.

The Shan represent the largest ethnic minority group in Burma. Especially in northern Shan State, along the China-Burma border, innocent villagers often have been caught in the crossfire between the Burma Army and ethnic Shan militia. Aung Moung was among the hundreds of thousands of Shan who found refuge in Thailand. "No one was safe," he said.

Aung Moung (21), Chiang Mai, Thailand

"No one was safe."

FORCED TO FLEE

Arif (13), New Delhi, India

About one million Rohingya live in Burma, mostly in northern Arakan State. A Muslim ethnic group who speak an Indo-Aryan language and practice Islam, many Rohingya descend from families who have lived in Burma for generations. Viewed by Burma's government as "illegal Bengali," Rohingya are denied citizenship. Burma's 1982 Citizenship Act rendered them officially stateless. Today, Rohingya are unable to marry, travel outside their villages or repair their mosques without securing permits or paying bribes. Considered by the United Nations to be "one of the world's most persecuted minorities," hundreds of thousands of Rohingya have fled Burma, including many to India. In a workshop in a makeshift Rohingya encampment outside Delhi, Arif painted why he fled Burma. "I had never seen helicopters shoot bullets before."

"I had never seen helicopters shoot bullets before."

In June 2012, an outbreak of violence between Buddhists and Rohingya Muslims in Arakan State ignited long-simmering tensions between the communities. State security forces were unable or unwilling to quell the violence. In some cases, they were actively complicit. A week later, President Thein Sein declared a state of emergency. The following month he told the United Nations High Commission for Refugees (UNHCR) that the only solution was to send the Rohingya to UN-administered camps or to a third country. Within a year, 142,000 displaced people in Arakan State, the vast majority Muslims, had sought refuge in camps that segregated Buddhists and Muslims. Meanwhile, anti-Muslim violence spread beyond Arakan State, impacting Muslims with legal citizenship. Suddenly, Muslims nationwide lived in fear.

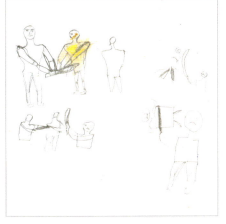

Top: Rofiqr (11) and Zuber (12); Bottom: Nooz Muhammad (13), Jannatara (12), New Delhi, India

FORCED TO FLEE

Ma Ei Lay (16), Mae Sot, Thailand

Ma Ei Lay's brother had been playing outside his school. His grandmother pleaded for the soldiers not to take him. "She hasn't been the same since," Mae Ei Lay said. Easy prey, children as young as 10 have been bought or abducted to fill the ranks of the Burma Army—and sometimes also ethnic armies. "Recruitment officers" have been known to falsify enlistment documents to register children as being at least 18 years old.

"I haven't seen my family since."

Ling Naing (21), New Delhi, India

"I was 15 when I joined the Chin National Army, as a porter." Ling Naing carried soldiers' equipment and food. After serving his duty, he returned to his village. There, the village elder urged him to flee to India. Having supported a "rebel" army, a target would be on his back. "I haven't seen my family since."

21

FORCED TO FLEE

San Lin Htay (16), Mae Sot, Thailand

"The rifle was heavy." It barely fit into the palm of San Lin Htay's hands. He had joined the Karen National Liberation Army to help protect his people—ethnic Karen —against the Burma Army. As he struggled to keep pace with his older comrades, his spirits were buoyed by visions of attending a school where he would be allowed to study the Karen language, culture and history.

"He could have been my brother."

His knees were buckling, eyes pleading, his entire body trembled. "He could have been my brother," Mu Paw Htay said. Abducted by Burma Army "recruitment officers" in his village, Mu Paw Htay had been taken to a remote training camp where he was programmed to kill his own people. That day, horrified by what he had become in the eyes of the Karen boy cowering before him, Mu Paw Htay dropped his rifle and ran and ran—all the way to Thailand.

Mu Paw Htay (14), Mae Sot, Thailand

FORCED TO FLEE

Many of Burma's most valuable natural resources are located in regions inhabited by the country's ethnic groups, which comprise more than a third of Burma's population. Often, government development projects have led to the forced eviction and relocation of entire ethnic villages and forced labor. "Children not much older than me had to miss school," nine-year-old Naom said.

Naom (9), Aizawl, Mizoram State, India

"Children not much older than me had to miss school."

May Yu Mon (15), New Delhi, India

The Burma Army has used sexual violence as a "weapon of war" to persecute and demoralize ethnic communities. Perpetrators are rarely held accountable. From Chin State, May Yu Mon wished that more women could be actively involved in peace negotiations. She was sure that more female voices would result in a significant decline in the number of women and girls being raped by soldiers.

FORCED TO FLEE

Metta Sutta
skilled in goodness   knows the path
gentle in speech   peaceful and calm
let none deceive another, or despise any being

Kyaw Soe Linn (33), New Delhi, India

"We still wonder what happened to the abbot."

As armed conflict continued in ethnic areas, the economic situation in urban areas deteriorated unexpectedly in 2007. In September of that year, the world's attention was riveted by videos of neverending columns of Buddhist monks streaming through the streets of Burma. Without warning, the ruling junta had removed all fuel subsidies, doubling the price of fuel and—in turn—everything transported, including food. Moved by the people's despair, tens of thousands of Buddhist monks took to the streets in protest, chanting the *Metta Sutta,* a prayer of loving kindness. Kyaw Soe Linn recalled how, a week later, soldiers swarmed the streets. The Internet was shut down. Dusk-to-dawn curfews were enforced. Monasteries were raided. Thousands of protestors were arrested. And monks vanished.

Ordained as a Buddhist monk shortly after reaching Thailand, Panya resided at a Shan temple in Chiang Mai. One of his earliest and most disturbing childhood memories was of the sudden disappearance of the abbot from his village's Buddhist temple. After attending a political meeting in Shan State, the abbot vanished. Villagers suspected the abbot had been arrested, but no one knew for sure. This episode left an indelible impression on Panya's sense of security in Burma. He never felt safe again. Years later, he jumped at an invitation to join his friends in Thailand. "We still wonder what happened to the abbot."

Panya (29), Chiang Mai, Thailand

This is what should be done by one who is skilled in goodness who knows the path of peace
let them be able and upright, straightforward and gentle in speech

FORCED TO FLEE

Zothansangi recalled how, in her native Chin State, Burma Army soldiers stole her family's chickens and pigs. When the soldiers returned, they took their home and land. It wasn't the first time, or the last. "After a while, you learn not to become attached."

Zothansangi (13), Aizawl, Mizoram State, India

Roluahpuia (16), New Delhi, India

Roluahpuia's father was working in the fields when it happened. Several Chin soldiers had stopped by their farm for some vegetables to eat and left a thank-you note. Burma Army soldiers patrolling the area discovered the note. When Roluahpuia's father returned from the fields later that evening, the Burma Army soldiers were waiting for him. They interrogated him about his ties to the Chin National Army. Around midnight, he managed to escape.

"After a while, you learn not to become attached."

FORCED TO FLEE

Fighting between the Burma Army and the Kachin Independence Army broke out in 2011, ending a 17-year ceasefire. Once again, thousands of innocent civilians were forced to flee their homes and take refuge in makeshift camps cut off from aid groups. Regardless of who fired the first shot, the ongoing military operations of the Burma Army contradicted the government's promise to protect civilians and ensure humanitarian access to vulnerable populations.

The very institution that waged war on the Kachin and other ethnic communities had institutionalized its power through the 2008 Constitution. Ethnic Kachin, Bawk Pa said, "How can the government defend a constitution that enables the military to operate above the law?"

Bawk Pa (24), Myitkyina, Kachin State, Burma

"How can the government defend a

Taas (16), Chiang Mai, Thailand

Taas was only one month old when his parents brought him to Thailand from Shan State. Most of what he knew about why his family left Burma he learned from his parents. No matter how hard they worked their farmland, they had been unable to save money. On an ongoing basis, his father had been forced to sell his cultivated rice to the Burma Army for below-market-value prices. Before Taas was born, his mother gave birth to a baby girl. When the baby fell ill and the family couldn't afford the trip to the hospital, she died. Taas' painting illustrates why they couldn't save money, why they couldn't save the baby.

constitution that enables the military to operate above the law?"

FORCED TO FLEE

Mon Hkur (15), Chiang Mai, Thailand

Burma is the world's second largest producer of opium, behind Afghanistan. In remote Shan State, the vast majority of townships are engaged in poppy cultivation, accounting for over 90% of Burma's total opium harvest. Drug trafficking is intimately linked to the national and ethnic armies. For impoverished farmers, opium provides a very profitable crop easily traded for cash, food, goods, guns or medicine. Mon Hkur's painting portrays how the greed of corrupt officials has fueled poppy production and drug addiction among Shan villagers. "The drug trade thrives on poverty and corruption," concluded Mon Hkur.

"The drug trade thrives on poverty and corruption."

Although Tiger was born in Chiang Mai, he was attuned to current events in Shan State. His painting expresses how he felt his family's homeland—represented by the Shan State flag—was pillaged and bled for the benefit of the Burman majority. Villagers feared that if they sought justice, Burma Army soldiers would retaliate.

Tiger (15), Chiang Mai, Thailand

FORCED TO FLEE

Jo Thang Lian Pa, New Delhi, India

Drafted by the former military junta, Burma's 2008 Constitution grants the military autonomy and supremacy over the quasi-civilian government. It reserves 25% of Parliamentary seats for military appointees, and constitutional amendments require more than 75% approval for passage. In essence, the military has veto power over changes to the constitution. Under these limitations, the civilian government lacks full sovereign powers as defined by international law. "Not until our constitution reflects the best interests of the people …," Jo Thang Lian Pa started, his voice trailing off.

"Not until our constitution reflects the best interests of the people…"

U Myint Htun's visual story depicts how, given the constraints of Burma's 2008 Constitution, President Thein Sein at times can appear to be two-faced, nodding at members of Parliament with one side of his face while smiling at those victimized by the military with the other side. President Thein Sein faces a diplomatic balancing act. Only when the 2008 Constitution has been overhauled to support genuine, sustainable democracy will the president be able to keep the military's cronies in check and foster national unity and peace.

U Myint Htun (former political prisoner), Mandalay, Burma

FORCED TO FLEE

Until a few years ago, Burma had one of the world's most repressive media environments. Exiled Burmese newsgroups relied on networks of underground video journalists (VJs) to smuggle their reports out of the country. The documentary *Burma VJ: Reporting from a Closed Country* chronicles the bravery of VJs during the 2007 Saffron Revolution. Their video footage broadcast via satellite back into Burma and around the world. Thanks to this continuous loop of images, Burma's military regime realized the world was watching. While helping keep the death toll from the 2007 protests down, underground VJs, bloggers and other media activists paid a price. When caught, they were dealt lengthy prison sentences.

A Chin girl, Aizawl, Mizoram State, India

Lao Kham (21), Chiang Mai, Thailand

Throughout Burma, especially in remote ethnic regions, good ideas have been suppressed or discouraged, if not punished.

In 1990, Aung San Suu Kyi's opposition party, the National League for Democracy (NLD), won 82% of the seats in Parliament. However, the military regime refused to relinquish its power. Instead, it kept Aung San Suu Kyi under house arrest and sentenced numerous members of her party to prison. Unaware of their rights, the people of Burma often have been afraid to think and speak freely. Lao Kham left Shan State to share his concerns and ideas openly. "I was tired of being muzzled by my own fears."

"I was tired of being muzzled by my own fears."

"WHAT DO YOU REMEMBER MOST ABOUT YOUR JOURNEY TO SAFETY?"

LIFE AS A REFUGEE IS DEFINED BY UNCERTAINTY. Most refugees are unsure of their destination or whether they will ever be able to return home. Their journey to safety can be rife with danger. Often, they must endure long periods without proper nutrition, health care, shelter or education.

Some refugee youth travel with an adult caregiver. Others travel alone or with other children, separated from family or orphaned by an outbreak of conflict. As the visual stories in this chapter illustrate, it isn't uncommon for youth traumatized by violence or persecution to demonstrate profound resilience and courage. Often the "key" to finding refuge and adapting to a foreign environment and culture is an irrepressible faith or hope.

However, rarely does "refuge" mean a home away from home. Usually it is an overcrowded refugee camp or an impoverished, crime-infested urban slum, and not always a safer environment than the one left behind.

IN BURMA, THERE ARE MORE THAN 135 DIFFERENT ETHNIC GROUPS, each characterized by their own history, culture and language. The largest group is Burman (Bamar); they represent nearly 70% of the country's 51 million people. The other major ethnic groups include the Arakan (Rakhine), Chin, Kachin, Karen, Karenni, Mon and Shan. Burma's seven "states" are named after these ethnic groups; Burma's seven "divisions" are inhabited primarily by Burmans.

THE VAST MAJORITY OF REFUGEES FROM BURMA ARE ETHNIC PEOPLE who have fled civil war and persecution in the mountains and resource-rich border areas. Where they seek refuge depends upon which neighboring country is most accessible and welcoming.

Nearly all refugees are hosted by bordering countries. For the 1% of refugees who are selected to resettle in a third country, it can take years, if not decades, to reach their final destination and begin to develop a renewed sense of belonging.

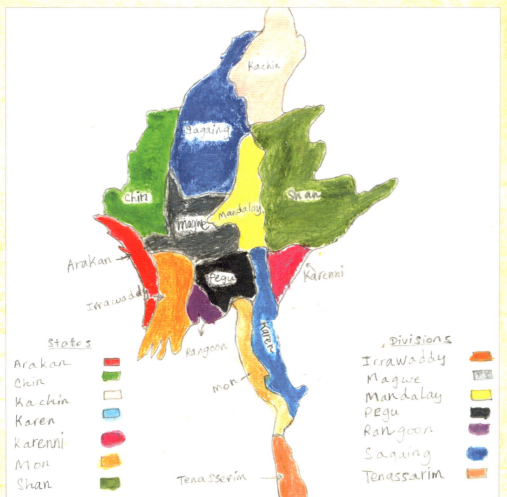

Tay Say (23), Kent, Washington, United States

JOURNEY TO SAFETY

Saw Yar Zar (16), Mae Sot, Thailand

Saw Yar Zar signed his visual story, on the reverse, with this tiny self-portrait (enlarged 800% here). "Night was our best friend," he said, and then explained that it was safest to flee under the cover of darkness. During the day, Burmese soldiers patrolling the area would be on the lookout. From sunrise until sundown, Saw Yar Zar huddled in a patch of tall grass, holding his trembling breath, praying.

"Night was our best friend."

Soldiers from the Karen National Liberation Army escorted Kyaw Eh's family as they made the long trek on foot to the Thai-Burma border. As a new day dawned, they counted their blessings. This time, they had only one casualty.

Kyaw Eh (19), Mae Sot, Thailand

JOURNEY TO SAFETY

Wah Ler Htoo revered the giant teak (*kyun*, in Burmese) leaves that sheltered his family and other villagers as they trudged through the jungle on their journey to the Thai-Burma border. Dried teak leaves had also served as roof "shingles" on his family's stilted bamboo hut in Karen State. Wah Ler Htoo's village had been torched by the Burma Army. Just across the border, his family found refuge in Mae La. The camp housed 45,000 refugees in bamboo thatched huts with—Wah Ler Htoo said, smiling—teak leaf roofs.

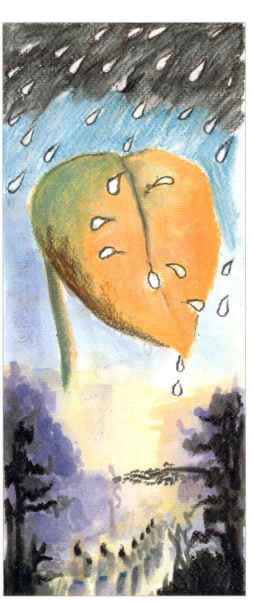

Wah Ler Htoo (17), Mae La refugee camp, Thailand

Zaw Zaw Htet (17), Mae Sot, Thailand

Zaw Zaw Htet was described as a serious student. While he studied at a migrant school and lived in an adjoining dormitory in Mae Sot, his mother stayed with his little brother and sister in a refugee camp several hours away by bus. "I am the reason my mother left Burma," he said. "She wanted what was best for me, for our family, for me to get an education."

"I am the reason my mother left Burma."

JOURNEY TO SAFETY

Naw Laura Shee (16), Mae Sot, Thailand

Migrant schools have operated in Thailand for several decades. In Tak Province, where the Thai-Burma border town of Mae Sot is located, over 70 migrant schools provide education for around 13,000 children of migrant workers from Burma, who number approximately three million in Thailand. As they trekked toward the border, Naw Laura Shee's mother stirred her and her brother's imaginations with visions of a quality education. "That's why we left, so we could dream."

"That's why we left, so we could dream."

Nor Oo (12), Mae Sot, Thailand

In the mid-1960s, the Burma Army imposed a brutal counter insurgency policy—called Four Cuts—on ethnic communities. Their goal? To cut ethnic armies' access to food, funds, intelligence and new recruits from sympathetic ethnic villagers. Targeting villages suspected to have familial ties to ethnic armies, soldiers forced villagers at gunpoint to choose: flee, fight or join the Burma Army. The rash of pillaged and burned villages in eastern Burma is a direct result of the policy. Like many other children, Nor Oo preferred to picture the Burma his grandparents reminisced about rather than the Burma they were forced to flee.

JOURNEY TO SAFETY

Yan Naing Win (18), Mae Sot, Thailand

It took Yan Naing Win four days. When he finally reached the Thai-Burma border, his eyes welled up with tears. He had left behind his family and village, the only home he had ever known. In Mae Sot, his visions of a brighter, bolder future began to take shape. On his first day of school, Yan Naing Win vowed to work hard, harder than he had ever worked before.

Yan Naing Win (18), Mae Sot, Thailand

Yan Naing Win was the first student to show up at our workshop, and the last to leave. He had traveled to Thailand by himself. As he approached the Thai-Burma border, he pictured his life after finding a place to live, after graduating from high school, after fulfilling his obligation to the Karen National Liberation Army … when he could finally pursue his lifelong dream of becoming an artist. As Yan Naing Win helped pack up our art supplies, I slipped a box of watercolor crayons and a box of watercolor pencils into his backpack.

JOURNEY TO SAFETY

Nyan Thar Myint (13), Mae Sot, Thailand

It can take villagers years to save up enough money to pay an agent to smuggle their child across the border to a better life in Thailand. All too often a child's expectations of finding a safe place to live and attending school are derailed by traffickers eager to usher unsuspecting youth into slave labor or the sex trade. Nyan Thar Myint knew students whose journeys to Mae Sot had been longer, much longer, than his. "I was lucky."

"I was lucky."

Tar Eh Soe (19), Mae Sot, Thailand

Human rights abuses and a shortage of jobs in Burma combined with higher wages in bordering countries have led to the migration of millions of ethnic people. Once migrant families have reached Mae Sot, their children become particularly vulnerable to human traffickers. Because they work all day, many parents can't watch their children. Also, in poor families it is common for children to work too. So when a broker offers to pay parents money, each month, to take their child to Bangkok to sell flowers, parents don't consider it human trafficking—unless they never see their child again.

JOURNEY TO SAFETY

Van Hlu Pui (19), Aizawl, Mizoram State, India

"I grew up on fear." Van Hlu Pui was harassed repeatedly by soldiers who would unexpectedly and repeatedly appear in her otherwise peaceful village in Chin State. She knew of women, even young girls, who had been raped by soldiers, so her fears spiked one day when a soldier from the Burma Army demanded that she, a lifelong Christian, kneel before him and quote Buddhist scriptures. She felt like she was being poked at gunpoint to the end of a plank. Today, Van Hlu Pui lives across the Indo-Burma border in mountainous Mizoram State, known for its picturesque beauty and for having a literacy rate of over 90%. "Mizoram" derives from "Mizo," the name of the local ethnic group that shares cultural and linguistic roots with the Chin of Burma.

"I grew up on fear."

Primarily subsistence farmers, 73% of the population of Chin State live below the poverty line. Why is their plight largely unknown? Until recently, the Burmese government restricted foreign access to Chin State and the Indian government restricted foreign access to neighboring Mizoram State—where about 100,000 mostly "illegal" Chin migrants have sought refuge. Reading a report about the vulnerable Chin population in Mizoram State prompted our trip there. When checked into our hotel, the manager said that we were required to register at Mizoram Police Headquarters within 24 hours. The next morning, an officer questioned us for about an hour about our family's reasons for visiting India's remote northeastern state. Only 1,100 foreigners had visited the entire state of Mizoram in the past 12 years.

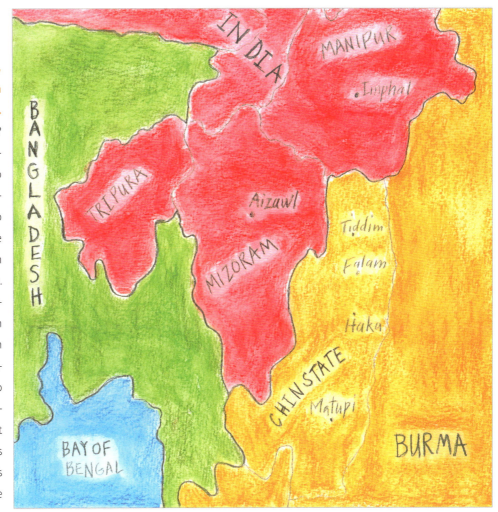

JOURNEY TO SAFETY

Annit (20), Aizawl, Mizoram State, India

Being registered by UNHCR as a refugee bestows numerous benefits, including legal status. However, most Chin cannot afford the lengthy and complicated journey to Delhi, the only place refugees are able to register in India. Starting in Chin State, many of those with sufficient means travel by jeep or on foot through a series of armed checkpoints before reaching the Indo-Burma border … across the river by boat to Mizoram State … by car to Mizoram's capital, Aizawl … by bus to the capital of neighboring Assam State, Guwahati … then finally by overnight train to Delhi. Annit had made the first three legs of the journey. Years later, she was still saving up for the last two.

Bawi Tha Sung (23), Aizawl, Mizoram State, India

Like most Chin in Burma, Bawi Tha Sung's family had worked in the fields. Being repeatedly forced to work for the Burma Army without pay had limited his family's ability to tend to their livestock and farm and maximize crop yields. At the same time, Bawi Tha Sung, a lifelong Christian, often faced religious persecution. About 90% of Chin State's population is Christian. Yet several important Christian landmarks have been destroyed and replaced by Buddhist pagodas, monasteries and statues. In Mizoram, India's most Christian state, Bawi Tha Sung was able to practice his religion openly. However, he was accused of stealing jobs from Mizo, who called him "illegal" and threatened to have him deported. "Still, life here is better than in Burma."

"Still, life here is better than in Burma."

JOURNEY TO SAFETY

Thousands of displaced and desperate Rohingya—fleeing deadly clashes between Buddhists and Muslims in Burma's Arakan State—have boarded smugglers' boats in the Bay of Bengal in search of refuge in a neighboring country. Hundreds have died of dehydration or starvation during the journey or drowned when their boats were capsized by turbulent seas. Or they have been sold to traffickers. Amid evidence of boats carrying Rohingya being pushed back out to sea by some countries, UNHCR has urged states in the region to keep their borders open to those in need of protection and to offer assistance until long-term solutions can be found.

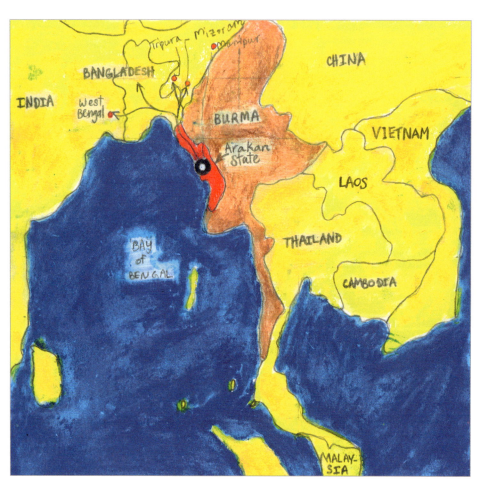

Ta Say (23), Kent, Washington, United States

"For now, this is home."

Jafar Alam (22), New Delhi, India

In June 2012, Jafar Alam fled violent riots that had erupted between Arakan Buddhists and Arakan Muslims in Arakan State. When he and his seamates discovered that Bangladesh was closed to Rohingya, they continued on to India. South of Delhi, beside a garbage dump, they—and over 200 other Rohingya—set up camp in a wide open field. Jafar translated at our visual storytelling workshop, which took place on a dirt field skirting the encampment. "For now, this is home."

JOURNEY TO SAFETY

Salam (13), Cox's Bazar refugee camp, Bangladesh

In the 1970s, the Burmese military launched a series of campaigns to "cleanse" the nation of Rohingya. Operation King Dragon was initiated in 1978 to identify and expel "illegal immigrants" in Burma. Over the next three months, nearly 250,000 Rohingya fled north to Bangladesh. In 1991, another military campaign, Operation Clean and Beautiful Nation, spurred a second mass exodus of some 200,000 Rohingya across the border. While many Rohingya have repatriated, nearly 250,000 continue to live in makeshift camps along the border. Salam was born and raised in Cox's Bazar, the refugee camp where a 19-year-old Rohingya boy named Zakir volunteered to facilitate a visual storytelling workshop. This visual story was painted in Zakir's workshop, which took place in his family's hut with five younger Rohingya boys.

"It was the scariest night of my life."

Siang Tha Dim (11), Tukwila, Washington, United States

"It was the scariest night of my life," Siang Tha Dim recalled. None of them knew how to swim. Nor had they been in a boat before. No matter how far down they crouched, they still felt like they were about to capsize and tumble into the oily black waters. As their boat drifted downstream, bolts of lightning crackled overhead. Siang Tha Dim's heart raced while her body froze, paralyzed by the realization that the same flash of lightning that had illuminated their route may have exposed them to soldiers patrolling the riverbank.

57

JOURNEY TO SAFETY

Vung It said she belonged to the Zomi tribe. Her family fled Chin State when she was a young girl. In Malaysia, she tried her hardest to avoid calling attention to herself. Every time someone gave her a second glance or asked her a question—which she couldn't understand, as she didn't speak the local language, Bahasa—she panicked. Her family was undocumented. "At any moment, we could have been deported."

Vung It (18), Tukwila, Washington, United States

"At any moment, we could have been deported."

Mary Niang (21), Tukwila, Washington, United States

Mary also identified as ethnic Zomi, from Chin State. Their family farm rolled over the mountains. "It was the most beautiful place I've ever lived," Mary said, using a fingertip to dab her painting with bright green watercolor. Whenever soldiers with the Burma Army came to her village, they would pillage the farm and demand 50% of her family's income. Once, they took her father with them; he was never seen or heard from again. Afraid of what might happen next, Mary's family fled, leaving behind their home, land and the only livelihood they had ever known. At the time, Mary was nine years old. After qualifying for refugee status in New Delhi, India, they were resettled in an urban area of the United States, where they have worked and studied hard to rebuild their lives.

JOURNEY TO SAFETY

Ta Say (23), Kent, Washington, United States

Ta Say resettled in the ethnically diverse community of Kent, a one-hour drive south of Seattle. A dedicated student, Ta quickly learned English and earned his way into the University of Washington, where he studied to become a social worker. Fluent in three languages, Ta worked as an interpreter for two refugee resettlement agencies. After school, he was a youth leader at his Karen church. Ever-resourceful, Ta secured a fellowship to help facilitate local visual storytelling workshops with refugees from around the world and paint maps for this book.

The Karen refugee girl behind this self-portrait grew up reinventing her identity—first in Thailand, and then again in Canada. No matter how much practice she had straddling her ethnic and "host" cultures, feeling whole again didn't get any easier.

A Karen girl, Langley, British Columbia, Canada

JOURNEY TO SAFETY

The refugee resettlement process can last months, years or decades. Ciang's family was originally from Chin State. After being granted refugee status and approved for resettlement in the United States, they were processed by the Department of State and the Department of Homeland Security. Then they were assigned to a re-settlement agency, flown to Seattle and provided with short-term assistance. While adapting to the local culture, refugee youth can lose touch with their cultural heritage, a concern shared by refugee elders for whom ethnicity is especially integral to their identity and daily life. This concern is heightened when refugees don't feel welcome in the larger community, causing many youth to feel torn between trying to "fit in" and honoring their roots. Ciang felt lucky. Her family was resettled in an ethnically diverse community. "We feel most at home Sundays, at church."

Ciang (33), Tukwila, Washington, United States

"We feel most at home Sundays, at church."

Hsar Kaw (17), Kent, Washington, United States

The 1% of refugees who are registered by UNHCR and accepted by a third country receive resettlement services to promote self-sufficiency and cultural adjustment. In the United States a case worker greets refugees at the airport and sets them up in an apartment. They receive a social security number, enabling them to apply for a job and enroll their children in school. A follow-up medical exam familiarizes them with local health services. Expected to find a job within six months of arrival, working-age refugees receive English language instruction. After living in a refugee camp along the Thai-Burma border, Hsar Kaw's parents were overwhelmed by the cost of living as well as by the complicated health care and educational "systems" in the United States. At first, everything was confusing—American culture was as foreign as the English language.

JOURNEY TO SAFETY

Kyaw Zaw Tun (12), Oakland, California, United States

The limited education of many refugee parents can slow the progress of their school-age children. In addition to not being able to help their children with their studies, refugee parents—while proud of their children's ability to adjust quickly—can feel sidelined. By the time refugee youth graduate from high school, they can be better prepared than their parents to secure a job. Having worked hard both at school and at home, where they translate for elders and tutor younger siblings, high-school graduates can be faced with a difficult decision: Do I work full-time to support my family, or pursue a college education and my dreams? Always, family comes first. Kyaw Zaw Tun recalled his family's first parent-teacher conference in his new school. "We didn't understand a word the teacher said."

Key Nay Htoo (18), Kent, Washington, United States

Refugees are commonly described as resilient. However, many of those who have been resettled in a free and democratic society struggle with post-traumatic stress, flashbacks, nightmares, insomnia and self-blame. The stigma associated with mental health issues among many refugees has discouraged refugees from seeking counseling or psychiatric treatment. Instead, they continue to suffer secretly, sometimes for the rest of their lives, behind a smile.

"We didn't understand a word the teacher said."

"WHAT IS IT LIKE TO LIVE IN EXILE?"

FOR THOSE WHO HAVE FLED PERSECUTION due to their ethnicity or religion, being discriminated against in the communities in which they have found refuge or been resettled can be a traumatic reminder of why they were forced to flee in the first place.

MOST REFUGEES LONG TO RETURN TO THE LAND OF THEIR ANCESTORS. However, deciding when to repatriate is never easy; refugees can feel torn. Even if a ceasefire agreement has been signed and tensions between the Burma Army and the ethnic army in their native state have eased, democratic reforms implemented by Burma's new quasi-civilian government have done little to improve the lives of ethnic communities. In fact, in many ethnic areas, human rights abuses have continued unabated.

At the same time, living for years—if not decades—in a refugee camp, cut off from their cultural roots, can feel like purgatory. As recipients of aid, refugees in camps are denied work permits. Eager to further their families' lives, many gamble on securing employment outside the camps, risking arrest, deportation or exploitation at the hands of corrupt officials. At the same time, many urban refugees don't receive aid and are exploited by employers.

For refugees registered by UNHCR in a neighboring country, familiarity with the local language and culture is key to adapting. It's not uncommon for refugees to be discriminated against and recoil from the larger "host" community into their exiled communities. Living among established refugees who share the same ethnicity and religion can ease the transition of newly resettled refugees while helping to preserve their cultural traditions.

* the leaves and the branches of bamboo plant are scratching, hitting, and beating on the groud the front of the small hut-monastery.

* but....... they are just ..... shades.

Aung Nan (26), ethnic Kachin from Khutkai, Shan State, Burma

WHETHER RESETTLED IN A NEIGHBORING COUNTRY OR IN A THIRD COUNTRY, in order for refugees to begin to feel at home, first they must feel welcome. Hopefully, the stories in this book will encourage readers to step out of their comfort zone and extend a hand. As the youths' paintings illustrate, there is a story of courage, resilience and determination behind each refugee, a story worthy of compassion and respect.

This chapter concludes with visual stories by several former political prisoners. Their paintings offer rare glimpses into the inner lives of political prisoners and illustrate that—in a country that has yet to honor the courage, vision and sacrifices of those who have paved the way for its freedom—once a political prisoner, always a political prisoner … yet another form of exile.

LIVING IN EXILE

The red triangles on this map plot the nine UNHCR-sponsored refugee camps along the Thai-Burma border. The first camps opened in the 1980s. Ever since, they have served as a safe haven for refugees fleeing violent conflict, especially in ethnic regions of eastern Burma. Despite recent democratic reforms in Burma and the signing of ceasefire agreements between the Burma Army and most ethnic armies, about 129,000 refugees continue to live in the camps, including about 40,000 who arrived too late to be eligible for resettlement abroad. Now is a time of heightened uncertainty. Talk of repatriation has stirred up anxieties among refugees who still have a well-founded fear of persecution if forced to return to Burma.

"Now, I don't want to forget."

Ta Eh Poe (16), Mae Sot, Thailand

As young Ta Eh Poe picked his way through the dense jungle toward the Thai-Burma border, atrocities he had witnessed flashed before him. The harder he tried to shut out the images, the more real, the more disturbing, they became. That was several years ago. Since then, his memories of that day—the day he was forced to flee his village—have faded. Fingering the lines of his painting, Ta Eh Poe turned to our translator and said, "Now, I don't want to forget." That was all that remained of Eh Poe's home: his memory.

LIVING IN EXILE

Nyan Thar Myint (13), Mae Sot, Thailand

Despite being guarded by armed Thai soldiers, camps along the Thai-Burma border are refugee-administered; residents build their own bamboo huts and camp leaders are elected by camp residents, democratically. Asked about his first impression of Umpiem Mai refugee camp, Nyan Thar Myint mused, "It was the most beautiful place I had ever seen." After a reflective pause, he added, "For the first time, I felt safe."

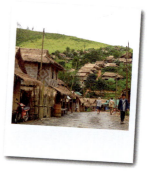

"For the first time, I felt safe."

Yan Naing Win (18), Mae Sot, Thailand

Pyae Wai Wai Hein (23), Mae Sot, Thailand

John Tuang (18), Umpiem Mai refugee camp, Thailand

Saw A., Umpiem Mai refugee camp, Thailand

LIVING IN EXILE

Lack of an education can stunt a child's future. The Thai border town of Mae Sot, also known as "Little Burma," is home to about 200,000 refugees and migrants from Burma. The chance to find higher paying work is a major draw. However, the job market in Mae Sot can be competitive. Some parents must travel further afield in Thailand to secure work. They send money back to pay for their children's room and board and schooling. In Mae Sot, children who have fled conflict and persecution in Burma quickly learn that, to help free their country, first they must free their minds.

"For me freedom means freedom of education."

LIVING IN EXILE

Even after crossing the border into Thailand and resettling in Nu Po refugee camp, Saw Yar Zar continued to feel as if he was being watched by Burma's then military junta; when he was forced to flee his village, the junta was called, ironically, the State Peace and Development Council. The SPDC stomped on anyone who dared question its authority. Saw Yar Zar recalled what it was like to live in Nu Po: "It felt like prison … Only we didn't do anything wrong and didn't know the length of our sentence."

Saw Yar Zar (16), Mae Sot, Thailand

"It felt like prison …"

*Paw Wah Htoo (19),
Mae Sot, Thailand*

*Klo Phillip (17),
Kent, Washington,
United States*

*Naw New Aye (21),
Mae Sot, Thailand*

*Klo Phillip (17),
Kent, Washington,
United States*

LIVING IN EXILE

Checkpoints set up by Thai authorities around Chiang Mai reminded Noom Harn of checkpoints pervasive in Burma. In Shan State, the designated "black zones" were off limits to tourists. In Chiang Mai, the checkpoints snagged undocumented migrants who fueled the local economy with cheap labor.

Noom Harn (19), Chiang Mai, Thailand

While many Shan have fled to Thailand, most continue to live in Shan State, an area rich in teak, gold, gemstones and opium. Sai Num's visual story contrasts his life before and after migrating to Chiang Mai. In Shan State, he said, villagers often felt like they were drowning in a sea of blood. In Thailand, even though the rule of law is more respected, Shan migrants can feel exploited by greedy employers and corrupt officials. While Sai Num felt freer and happier as a migrant worker in Chiang Mai, he still felt he was trapped in a dark place. "At least I know what freedom looks like now."

Sai Num (24), Chiang Mai, Thailand

"At least I know what freedom looks like now."

LIVING IN EXILE

Sai Sai was the middle child in a family of five children. After his mother passed away, Sai Sai and all of his brothers and sisters moved to different parts of Thailand to find work. Staying behind in Shan State, Sai Sai's father lived alone in a poor, yet peaceful, village. Sai Sai imagined his father seated outside his small hut, worrying about his five children, strewn across Thailand, fending for themselves. Every month, Sai Sai sent as much of his meager salary as he could spare back to his father.

Sai Sai (21), Chiang Mai, Thailand

Jarm Mon (23), Chiang Mai, Thailand

Children can be cruel, especially to children who are "different." After migrating from Shan State to Chiang Mai, Jarm Mon was enrolled in a Thai school. She recalled being teased and bullied by her Thai classmates. They called her names and poked fun at her accent, knowing she wouldn't defend herself. Recess was the hardest. There was no place to hide. "When the teachers pretended nothing was wrong, I felt even more alone."

"When the teachers pretended nothing was wrong, I felt even more alone."

LIVING IN EXILE

Lalramnghaka (25), Aizawl, Mizoram State, India

The Chin comprise 10% of the population of India's far northeastern Mizoram State, where rising tensions between Mizo and Chin have sparked outbreaks of violent conflict. "Mizos think democracy has already come to Burma," said Lalramnghaka. "They say it's time for us to leave." As most Mizos and Chins are Christian, church groups have tried to nurture a sense of kinship between the communities, reminding Mizos that they share a common history and ethnic ancestry with the Chin. The host of the visual storytelling workshop Lalramnghaka attended made a point of inviting several local Mizo women to join us, and ceremoniously thanked them for their participation.

Even though they felt marginalized by the resentment and animosity of local Mizos, Chin who participated in our visual storytelling workshops in Mizoram's mountainside capital—Aizawl—couldn't imagine returning to Chin State any time soon. Working Monday through Saturday enabled them to be financially self-sufficient. And regularly attending a local Chin church, one of many in Aizawl, had fostered their shared sense of belonging and purpose.

Bo Thut, Aizawl, Mizoram State, India

"They say it's time for us to leave."

LIVING IN EXILE

Moe Moe Khine, an ethnic Chin refugee, explained that her father couldn't take care of their family. He couldn't get a job. No one would hire him. He was discriminated against for having AIDS. So Moe Moe Khine and her baby brother, who was happy to cuddle in her lap throughout our workshop, made the long trek from Chin State to Delhi. Moe Moe Khine said she was lucky. She was able to find work and earn enough to send money back to her father in Burma. She prayed for his health. She hadn't heard from him in a while. She said, "Not knowing if he's still alive makes me even more homesick."

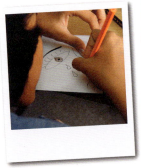

Moe Moe Khine (17), New Delhi, India

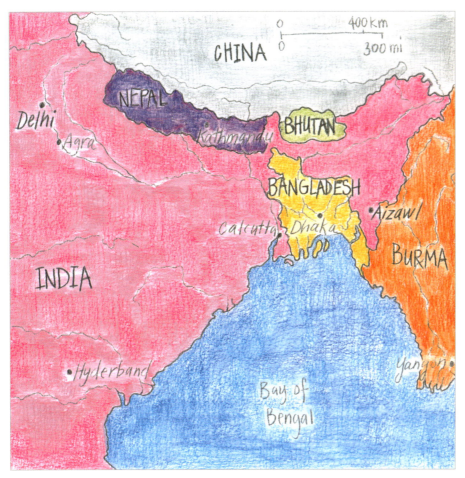

Inhabitants of the underdeveloped northeastern region of India, including Mizoram State, often migrate to mainland India in search of higher education and higher-paying jobs. Remote and commonly misunderstood, northeastern India is thought by many mainlanders to be a site of infiltration, attracting terrorists scheming to establish an independent Christian state in Christian-dominated regions of the northeast. Such perceptions have helped justify discrimination and violent attacks against northeasterners resettled in the greater Delhi area, including Chin refugees and migrants who share the facial features of the Mizo people.

"Not knowing if he's still alive makes me even more homesick."

LIVING IN EXILE

Jimmy (26), New Delhi, India

The chance to register with UNHCR-Delhi as a refugee is a popular dream among Chin. Being registered with UNHCR bestows benefits, including access to affordable housing, education and health care. Of the Chin refugees living in the greater Delhi area, about 8,000 are registered; several thousand more are unregistered. Either way, refugees are at the mercy of locals—often impoverished themselves—who can resent foreign competition for jobs and limited resources. During the sweltering summers, community faucets occasionally run dry. City water trucks come to the rescue. Jimmy said, "Even if we get there first, we always end up last in line."

Joseph (17), New Delhi, India

Thousands of Chin refugees pack into tiny rented rooms in the fly-infested alleyways of Bodella, an impoverished refugee enclave in West Delhi. No one else looked twice when Joseph, the lanky teenage son of the Chin pastor who hosted our workshop at his church, entered the room in dark shades and a bandana wrapped around his head like a turban. Walking home from a job interview, Joseph had been beaten up by three drunk Indians who then stole his bag, wallet and mobile phone. Thankfully, the auto rickshaw driver who found him crumpled up in the middle of the road, vomiting blood, his head cut open and eyes swollen shut, was kind.

"Even if we get there first, we always end up last in line."

LIVING IN EXILE

May Yu Mon looked shell-shocked. It happened while she was working in a factory. She was raped by an Indian co-worker. What could she do? She didn't speak Hindi. Besides, she knew her employer would side with her co-worker; she was dispensable. So each day May Yu Mon returned to the factory. She had to; her family in Chin State depended upon her income. Two weeks before our workshop, she finally found another job. Later, I asked May Yu Mon about her dream for the future. Her face lit up. The question had inspired a vision. She dreamed of opening a rape crisis center for refugee women and girls in Delhi.

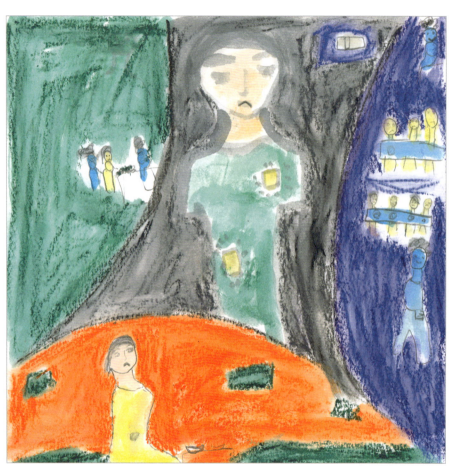

May Yu Mon (15), New Delhi, India

Biak Hlawn Tha (8), New Delhi, India

Workshop participants in the Delhi area said they were accustomed to racist slurs. One Chin participant said, "We're called *Chinki*," a derogatory term which means "a small opening," referring to the shape of northeasterners' eyes. The host of one of our workshops in Delhi, and from the northeast herself, Dr. Alana Golmei said, "Nobody will come as our savior to help us." Whether advocating on behalf of survivors, presenting at conferences, speaking to the media or rallying the support of legislators, Alana has tirelessly challenged institutionalized racism in Indian society. Founder of a helpline for rape survivors and others in distress from northeastern India, she is painfully aware of the costs of the continued neglect of this issue.

"Nobody will come as our savior to help us."

LIVING IN EXILE

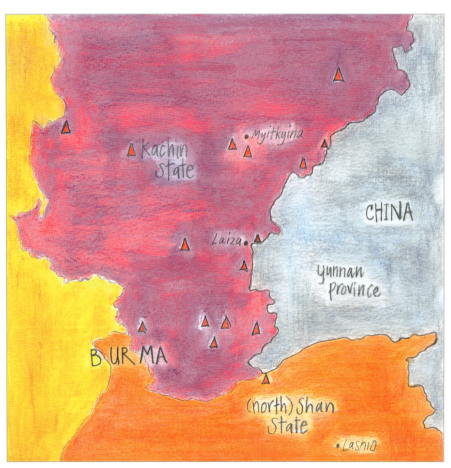

In Burma, there is a strong correlation between large-scale development projects and human rights violations. Kachin and Shan states are rich in natural resources. Bordering populous and resource-needy China and India, Burma's northern-most states have drawn scores of economic development projects led by Burmese and foreign companies cooperating with the Burma Army. The construction of hydroelectric dams, mines and pipelines has spurred land confiscations, the displacement of communities, extortion and forced labor. The red triangles on this map pinpoint the whereabouts of IDP camps in Kachin and northern Shan states, which provide refuge to over 100,000 ethnic people displaced by conflict between the Burma Army and the Kachin Independence Army (KIA). Primarily farmers, the greatest wish of most IDPs is to return to their land and once again be self-sufficient.

In a society that often blames the victim, women who have been raped or battered can carry feelings of shame and humiliation with them for the rest of their lives. This painting of an internally displaced Kachin woman is by an ethnic Shan refugee woman. Resettled in the United Kingdom, Feraya Ullathorne said, "I wanted to express my solidarity with women in conflict zones in Burma," women struggling to break cycles of violence and build peaceful communities.

Feraya Ullathorne, United Kingdom

"I wanted to express my solidarity with women in conflict zones in Burma."

LIVING IN EXILE

About 6,000 Rohingya asylum seekers have crossed Bangladesh to reach India. First they must pass through villages in Burma—a risky venture, as Rohingya are forbidden to travel between townships without official permission. A Rohingya asylee in Delhi said he had owned a farm in Arakan State. "After confiscating my land, the Burma Army picked me up on an extortion bid," he explained. That was the last straw. He said, "We came to India because it is the land of *raham-karam*," meaning "compassion and grace." (The red triangles to the right represent the IDP camps in Burma's northern Arakan State and the refugee camps in Bangladesh's Cox's Bazar district.)

Muhammad Kabiv (11), New Delhi, India

This visual story was painted by a Rohingya child in a 222-person Rohingya encampment in southeast Delhi. Built on a plot of barren land, the camp was made up of some 50 tents, re-purposed tin sheets propped up on bamboo stilts. A local charity had lent the land to the Rohingya families after they were chased out of their prior camp, near UNHCR's office, a month earlier. As the toilet was an adjoining empty plot, women in the camp waited until nighttime to relieve themselves and bathe. They couldn't understand why UNHCR had turned them away; legal refugee status would have enabled their children to go to school. A grandfather said, "Wherever we go, we are chased away." He prayed that they would not outstay their welcome.

"Wherever we go, we are chased away."

LIVING IN EXILE

Ko Hlaing Bwa (former political prisoner), Mandalay, Burma

Prominent former political prisoners have asked the Burmese government to acknowledge the prior military government's wrongdoings. If the new quasi-civilian government condemns human rights abuses committed by its predecessors, they say, wouldn't more members of Parliament be committed to democratizing Burma's constitution? Currently, if political prisoners released from prison under an amnesty are convicted of another crime, such as protesting peacefully without authorization or "unlawful association," they could be required to serve not only a new prison term, but also the remainder of their prior, suspended sentence.

In Mae Sot, we visited the offices of the Assistance Association of Political Prisoners—Burma, the leading advocate of political prisoners in Burma. Stepping into AAPPB's adjoining museum, I was riveted by this image. As it turned out, it was painted by an artist who had organized our workshop at Sky Blue, an elementary school in Mae Sot city dump, where countless refugee families live and support themselves by digging for recyclables. To me, the painting honors the boundless sacrifices political prisoners and their families have made for Burma's freedom.

Nyan Soe, Mae Sot, Thailand

LIVING IN EXILE

Having befriended prison guards, political prisoner Zaw Zaw Lin "earned" unique privileges while in Mandalay Prison. Guards routinely swept outside his cell. Occasionally, concealed between the reeds of a guard's broom would be a blue ink cartridge, discreetly slipped through the bars of his cell. Zaw Zaw Lin used the ink and old, discarded prison shirts to secretly chronicle scenes from his imagination, pen short stories and create little illustrated books. Zaw Zaw Lin shared his 10 x 12 foot cell with three other political prisoners.

Zaw Zaw Lin (former political prisoner), Mandalay, Burma

"In prison, art was like when you go underwater, you need a regulator."

Zaw Zaw Lin and Htein Lin (former political prisoners), Mandalay, Burma

After our workshop with over 70 former political prisoners in Mandalay, I was introduced to one of Zaw Zaw Lin's cellmates, poet Maung Tin Thit. He said that another one of their cellmates was pioneering artist Htein Lin. "In prison, art was like when you go underwater, you need a regulator," Htein Lin has said. It kept him sane. To the left is a portrait of Zaw Zaw Lin painted by Htein Lin on a recycled prison shirt. The cellmates were released in 2004 after spending six and a half years behind bars. Zaw Zaw Lin became a Buddhist monk. To the left is a photograph of him taken shortly before he died in 2013.

LIVING IN EXILE

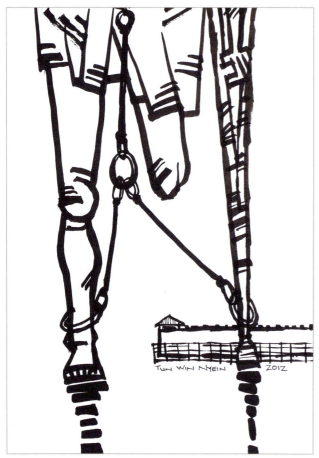

Tun Win Nyein (former political prisoner), Rangoon, Burma

The two pieces on this page are by artist Tun Win Nyein. We met in Rangoon at an art auction for the 8888 Uprising Silver Jubilee, a series of 25th anniversary events. Early the next morning we reunited at Tun Win Nyein's home. Former political prisoners, he and his wife, Hnin Hnin Hmway, showed us dozens of paintings by Rangoon-based former political prisoners. One piece, above, recalls Tun Win Nyein's time behind bars. He tracked the length of his imprisonment by tallying the number of visits he received from his family. The piece to the left honors his friend Myo Myint, a former Burma Army soldier who was tortured and imprisoned for 15 years for defecting and joining the democracy movement. Myo Myint's story is told in the documentary film, *Burma Soldier*.

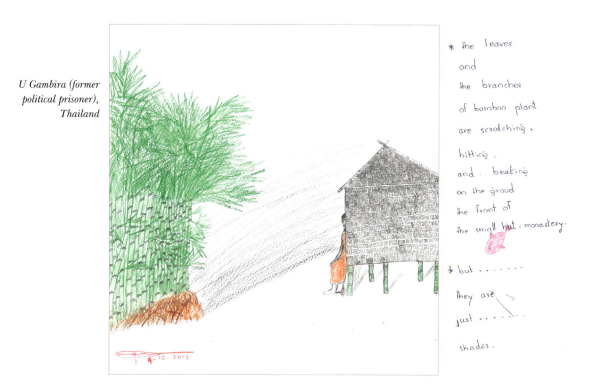

U Gambira (former political prisoner), Thailand

This visual story is by Nyi Nyi Lwin, better known as Ashin Gambira, an organizer of Burma's 2007 Saffron Revolution. After the military junta cracked down on the Saffron Revolution, Gambira was arrested, brutally beaten and sentenced to 68 years in prison. Like countless lesser-known political prisoners, the torture he sustained at the hands of his interrogators and jailers left him with traumatic brain injuries, chronic health problems and paralyzing flashbacks. Released from prison during a general amnesty in 2012, Gambira, a Burmese Buddhist monk since the age of 12, was locked out of his monastery … and every other monastery he tried to enter. Long-time friends, even his family doctor, were afraid to be associated with him. Despite being plagued by health issues, ostracized by former allies in the Sangha and monitored by state security forces, Gambira has continued to speak openly on behalf of those treated unjustly in Burma, including the Rohingya.

"WHAT DO YOU MISS MOST ABOUT YOUR NATIVE LAND?"

WHEN WORKSHOP PARTICIPANTS WERE ASKED what they missed most about their homeland, sometimes their eyes lit up and sometimes they turned misty. Recalling fond memories can be bittersweet.

Often, youth portrayed loved ones they had left behind. A bright young man who left Burma to find a job in India that would pay for his younger brother's education painted a heart-shaped picture of his parents. Despite sacrificing his own dreams of a higher education to support his family, he felt like he had abandoned them. "Whenever I feel happy here, I feel guilty that I'm not there."

Most youth—including children of refugees born along the borders of Burma and raised in exile—longed for the land of their ancestors. They painted a simpler, more peaceful way of life, reflective of elders' distant

Lal Biak Runga (22), New Delhi, India

memories. Once considered the "rice bowl of Asia," Burma had fallen from grace and been isolated from the rest of the world by over 50 years of military dictatorship. One refugee teenage girl said, "The place I miss most no longer exists."

THE END OF MILITARY RULE AND DEMOCRATIC REFORMS implemented by the new quasi-civilian government have opened doors to the outside world and accelerated change in Burma. While infusing the long-impoverished country with humanitarian aid and foreign investment, rapid changes—especially in ethnic regions of the country—have threatened the status quo and natural landscape.

Lalpekmawii (14), New Delhi, India

The visual stories in this chapter illustrate dual values widely shared by refugees, values that transcend age, ethnicity and religion: a sense of belonging and of self-sufficiency. Having survived or at least witnessed human rights abuses, exiles know all too well that only when these values are uniformly shared can an equitable set of rights and responsibilities be agreed upon.

And only when all of the people of Burma are guaranteed a voice at the table, a voice in how their country is governed, is a just, inclusive and lasting peace possible.

MEMORY

Jane Labiuatdik (12), New Delhi, India

Twelve-year-old Jane beamed as she handed me her visual story. At first glance, I saw a lovely family portrait. However, as I had come to expect, there was a backstory. Jane's parents had divorced. Her father had returned to Burma while her mother moved to India's northeastern Mizoram State. We were scheduled to travel to Mizoram the following day, so I asked Jane if we could deliver the painting to her mother. Or give her mother photos we had taken of Jane encircled by her friends in the workshop. Jane looked down at the painting, face up in her palms, but didn't say anything. Finally, she explained. She didn't have an address or a phone number for her mother, or for her father. She hadn't seen or heard from either of them since they left Delhi, two years earlier.

Phone Myint hosted our workshop at a home for young boys and girls who had been trafficked across the Thai-Burma border. The stilted shelter was guarded by dozens of chickens that squawked and flapped about as our shoes made slurping sounds through the muddy front yard and scaled the wooden steps that led up to the front porch. As we entered the main room, floorboards creaked beneath our bare feet. Several children were huddled around a meowing kitten in the far corner of the room. At once, they turned and smiled shyly. While being a father figure to the 10 children at the shelter hadn't relieved Phone Myint of his guilty conscience, he too had found a safe haven. Two years earlier he had been forced to flee his village in Burma. "My family doesn't know I'm alive." He prayed that keeping them in the dark would protect them from the Military Intelligence officers who had targeted his life for distributing anti-government pamphlets.

Phone Myint, Mae Sot, Thailand

"*My family doesn't know I'm alive.*"

101

MEMORY

With a decisive nod, Saw Myint Htoo held up his finished painting. His father had served in the Karen National Liberation Army, a symbol of his people's struggle for greater autonomy from the central government and increased control over the wealth of natural resources in Karen State. Over six decades, tens of thousands of Karen soldiers had sacrificed their lives in the name of freedom. Their heroic role commanded near universal respect from the Karen people. "We are Karen," Saw Myint Htoo asserted. Like other Karen youth in our workshops along the Thai-Burma border, Saw Myint Htoo was proud of his heritage.

Saw Myint Htoo (16), Mae Sot, Thailand

"Whenever I feel happy here, I feel guilty that I'm not there."

Bo Thut (31), Aizawl, Mizoram State, India

Bo Thut traveled by himself from Chin State to Aizawl, the capital of India's Mizoram State. He left behind his mother, father, brother … and, as his visual story suggests, his heart. Employed and housed by a large textile factory on the outskirts of town, Bo Thut sent money back to cover his younger brother's schooling and help with his family's living expenses. Years after moving to Mizoram, he continued to feel torn. "Whenever I feel happy here, I feel guilty that I'm not there."

MEMORY

Nanaye Seinou (30), Chiang Mai, Thailand

Ten years had passed since Nanaye Seinou, also known as "Pim," fled Burma. Pim missed her father, farm life and the natural beauty of the mountains in rural Shan State. The Shan State flag in the background of her visual story represents Pim's longing to be free and self-reliant in her homeland rather than needing to work in a foreign country where she felt like an unwelcome guest who needed to disguise her identity. The mother of a six-year-old daughter born in Thailand, Pim worked as a nanny for another family. While grateful for the opportunity to support herself and her daughter, Pim dreamed of returning home, opening a small business and introducing her daughter to the rest of her family, in Shan State.

"I paint to spread awareness globally."

Feraya Ullathorne, United Kingdom

Exiled Tai Shan people often say, *Tsai teung Merng Tai,* **which means "The heart yearns for Shan land."** Feraya was 14 years old when her family had to leave Burma. In her painting, Feraya reminisced about her family's summer holiday at a palace in Shan State. Before dinner, the court musicians would perform on the verandah. Feraya was six. Dressed in her court princess costume and headdress, Feraya would wait eagerly to dance the traditional dances. Today, Feraya paints internally displaced people from her motherland. "I paint to spread awareness globally."

MEMORY

Only after she was forced to flee Chin State, only after she had lost everyone and everything she held dearest, did Van Hlu Puii discover that home is more than a physical space. It's a sense of belonging. Van Hlu Puii's fondest memory and dream were one and the same: to rediscover a sense of feeling welcome. At the same time, she acknowledged, "The place I miss most no longer exists."

Van Hlu Puii (19), Aizawl, Mizoram State, India

"The place I miss most no longer exists."

Hani Kyaw (9), Mae Sot, Thailand

From downtown Mae Sot it took 15 minutes on the back of a motorcycle and down a pocked dirt road to reach Sky Blue. The little elementary school for migrant children from Burma was dwarfed by mountains of garbage. It wasn't until I inhaled my first overpowering whiff of the foul-smelling trash that the reality of living 24/7 in a sea of rubbish began to sink in. After school, students of Sky Blue would race home, heave a child-height bag over their shoulder, grab a pick and then join their parents on the garbage heap, rummaging for their family's share of recyclable plastics and metals. Most of the especially vibrant visual memories in this chapter were painted by refugee children who, like Hani Kyaw, are from Sky Blue.

MEMORY

Aung Soe Moe (14), Mae Sot, Thailand

Aung Soe Moe's family fled an outbreak of gunfire between the Burma Army and the Karen National Liberation Army. His visual story illustrates that golden pagodas weren't exclusive to predominantly Buddhist regions of Burma; they also dotted the landscape of Christian-dominated regions, including in Aung Soe Moe's Karen State. In peaceful areas, the presence of the shimmering hilltop pagodas served as a subtle reminder of Burma's Buddhist leaning. However, in conflict areas where locals had been persecuted for practicing another religion, Buddha's omnipresence was a source of contention.

Ta Nu Nu, Mae Sot, Thailand

Ethnic Karen and Christian, Ta Nu Nu spent his early childhood in Burma. For him, the presence of Buddhist pagodas didn't feel intrusive; he associated Buddhism with loving kindness. In 2007, when tens of thousands of Buddhist monks rose up and streamed barefoot through the streets of Burma, chanting the *Metta Sutta*, impoverished people of all faiths in Burma believed the monks were standing up not just for Buddhists but for all of Burma's people. "We were grateful for the monks' courage."

"We were grateful for the monks' courage."

MEMORY

Candace recalled her childhood. When she was growing up, her Karen community revolved around a Christian church. In some areas of Karen State, students attending schools run by the government felt pressured into converting to Buddhism. According to Karen human rights activists, the Burmese government has used state resources to finance Buddhist pagodas, monasteries and Buddhist-centric schools while restricting the construction of churches.

Candace (30), Langley, British Columbia, Canada

Saw Lime (13), New Delhi, India

Saw Lime fled the initial outbreak of violence between Buddhists and Muslims in Arakan State in June 2012. She wondered, why had only Rohingya been forced to flee the country? She was born in Burma. So were her parents. In India, she began to learn about human rights. No child should have to ask, "Aren't we human too?" Painting the mosque near her home, Saw Lime was grateful. She knew that she and other Rohingya who had managed to reach India were better off than Rohingya living in the more remote IDP camps in Arakan State, surrounded by Buddhist villages. There they were unable to work, unable to go to school, unable to leave their camps, for fear of being attacked by Buddhist extremists or forcibly detained by authorities.

"Aren't we human too?"

MEMORY

Naw Pau Hke Klee (14), Mae Sot, Thailand

Even now with a ceasefire agreement signed by both the Burma Army and the local Karen army in place, refugees like Naw Pau Hke Klee are afraid to return to the site of their old villages. Ethnic areas along the Thai-Burma border are among the most heavily mined areas in the world. After burning down a village, the Burma Army often peppered the area with landmines to ensure the displacement of entire communities. Thankfully, hundreds of landmine survivors—soldiers and civilians alike—have been able to regain their mobility at Mae Sot's Mae Tao Clinic, which outfits amputees with custom-made prosthetic limbs.

Ei Lwin (13), Mae Sot, Thailand

Many refugees who live in remote rural areas of Burma are self-reliant; they live off the land. Ei Lwin painted herself working in the garden with her mother. Her family grew mangoes, jackfruit and bananas … until their village was attacked by the Burma Army. "I miss my mother," Ei Lwin said. Had her mother stayed behind in Burma? I wondered. Had she died? Among refugee youth who have survived repeated outbreaks of violence the loss of a parent is common. Later, I asked Ei Lwin if she would like to return to Burma one day. She nodded. "My heart belongs where my mother is buried."

"My heart belongs where my mother is buried."

MEMORY

Naw Mu Thaw (17), Mae Sot, Thailand

Par Ei Hpyu (13), Mae Sot, Thailand

Chit Hnin Haing (10), Mae Sot, Thailand

Family stories, like family traditions, are passed down from generation to generation. Chit Hnin Haing inherited her fond memories of Karen State from her grandparents. Older refugees living in camps along the Thai-Burma border have yearned to return to their native land. Recently, those visions have been tarnished by news of government-proposed industrial zones where former refugees would have few options other than to work as laborers in large factories. Lifelong farmers, the refugees simply want their land back, land confiscated by the Burma Army or the government. They want compensation for their homes, farms and livestock—whatever was destroyed or stolen from them. Our translator summed it up: "They want what is theirs."

"They want what is theirs."

MEMORY

Htway Nyo (16), Mae Sot, Thailand

When Htway Nyo was a young girl living in Karen State, her father would often find her daydreaming under a tree. He would scold her for not staying focused on her chores. Then he would smile. He couldn't help but appreciate her aspirations for herself and her younger brother. Htway Nyo didn't want to become a farmer; she wanted to be a student. Not just at any school, but at a school that respected her Karen heritage. One day, Htway Nyo's father announced that their family needed to leave Burma. Her dream finally came true—in a migrant school right across the border.

Biaknem Chin's family had found refuge in a slum where we had to watch our step—and our backs—and continually swat flies off our faces. Biaknem Chin missed what our daughter took for granted, a safe place to play. Moving from Chin State to Mizoram to Delhi, and continually having to pack up and say goodbye, makes it hard for refugee children to establish friendships. Between navigating a big city where they often are bullied, struggling to keep up in classes taught in a foreign language and helping elders who struggle with their own issues, leisure time is a luxury few refugee children can afford. Yet as the young refugees we worked with picked up watercolor crayons and started to paint, the stress of daily life seemed to melt away, testifying to the irrepressible resilience and hope of children.

Biaknem Chin, New Delhi, India

MEMORY

An explosion of Chinese-financed mega-projects in Burma's resource-rich ethnic areas has raised concerns about the country's natural environment. One project, in particular, has been a lightning rod for public opposition: the Myitsone hydro-electric dam project in Kachin State, where 70% of the population farms. The project was designed to supply electricity to China's southern Yunnan Province. Once built, the dam would impact everyone who relies on the Irrawaddy River, Burma's primary source of water. Completion of the dam could submerge over 60 villages, displace more than 10,000 people and lead to widespread deforestation and erosion of the riverbed. In 2011, newly elected President Thein Sein bowed to a public backlash over the dam's potential impact. He suspended construction, demonstrating the benefits of civic participation. Lal Ruat Puii smiled. "Deep pockets no longer always win."

Lal Ruat Puii (19), New Delhi, India

"Deep pockets no longer always win."

Khai Bawi (24), New Delhi, India; Ral uk Thang (13), New Delhi, India
Lal Cling Liana (22), New Delhi, India; Biak-Hlun Cen Hrang, New Delhi, India

For residents of the Irrawaddy delta region and the former capital city of Rangoon, there was life before, and life after, 2 May 2008, the day Cyclone Nargis tore through southern Burma. High-speed winds and a 12-foot (3.6-meter) surge of sea water killed over 130,000 people and three-fourths of the livestock, blew away 700,000 homes and flooded millions of acres of rice fields. Desperate cyclone survivors resorted to drinking from streams where corpses lay, bloated and decomposing. Buddhist monks, community members and other volunteers rushed in with clean drinking water, food and medical supplies. Former political prisoner Zarganar, Burma's most famous comedian, was later sentenced to 59 years in prison for openly criticizing the junta's sluggish response and resistance to international aid. On 10 May, the junta went ahead with a planned referendum on the new military-drafted constitution, demonstrating how little they cared about survivors' needs.

"WHAT IS YOUR DREAM FOR THE FUTURE?"

MANY WORKSHOP PARTICIPANTS GRAVITATED TOWARD THE QUESTION, "WHAT IS YOUR DREAM FOR THE FUTURE?"

It steered clear of painful memories from the past, sparking instead visions of a brighter future. Merely reflecting upon and freely discussing ways in which they could help shape their own and their country's future seemed to inspire confidence in the young storytellers.

While refugee youth who have been resettled abroad dream of becoming self-reliant and contributing to their new communities, most refugees living along the borders of Burma dream of returning to their native land. They picture themselves serving their people, usually as teachers or doctors, promoting democratic principles and reuniting with loved ones.

OFTEN, YOUTHS' DREAMS RELATE TO HUMAN RIGHTS ISSUES
they illustrated earlier in a workshop when answering the question, "Why were you forced to flee?" or "What is it like to live in exile?" Picturing themselves addressing such issues on behalf of their ethnic communities, motherland and fellow

Aung Min (12),
Mae Sot, Thailand

exiles emboldens their visual voices to "speak" truth to power.

As the youth committed their visions to paper and shared their stories, they discovered strengths they had developed while overcoming the never-ending challenges of being refugees, including courage, resilience, ingenuity and perseverance. Having grown up straddling geographic boundaries, they had learned—out of necessity—how to bridge different ethnicities, languages, traditions, even identities.

COLLECTIVELY, OVER 1,200 YOUTH PARTICIPATED in our visual storytelling workshops. Youth representing Burma's diverse ethnic and religious groups. Youth whose families had been uprooted from their ancestral lands and torn apart by outbreaks of violent conflict. Youth who had been conscripted into armies, trafficked, preyed on for sex, orphaned, persecuted, discriminated against, marginalized and, without exception, forced to flee.

Handed a piece of watercolor paper, a pencil and a box of watercolor crayons, these same youth rose up, eager to share their dreams, eager to be heard and—by the end of the workshop—eager to make a difference in the world. All we had to do was ask.

Jimmy (26), New Delhi, India

What is freedom?

Freedom is happiness
Freedom is fearless
Freedom is a mango tree
Freedom is breathing deeply
Freedom is recess,
      at school
Freedom is a flower
      in bloom
Freedom is still,
      like a pond
Freedom is an education
Freedom is having choices
Freedom is making
      your own decisions
Freedom is being self-sufficient
Freedom is creative
Freedom is returning home,
      safely
Freedom is being with family
Freedom is a bird in flight
Freedom is adventurous
Freedom is peace
Freedom is a dream
Freedom is a cloud
Freedom is playful
Freedom is inside our heart
      and mind
Freedom is loving
      and being loved
Freedom is my friend

HOPES & DREAMS

Aye Mi Mi Kyaw (12), Mae Sot, Thailand

I will never forget Aye Mi Mi Kyaw, the 12-year-old girl who painted this visual story.
We met in a stilted wooden shelter for young survivors of trafficking. Her entire right cheek was covered with scar tissue, as if from a serious burn. Out of the hundreds of youth who participated in our workshops along the Thai-Burma border, Aye Mi Mi Kyaw was the only child whose eyes remained lifeless when I asked if she had a dream for the future. Kneeling beside her, I remembered that half an hour earlier, she had returned from school with another little girl, named Hla Lay, now seated kitty-corner from her at the shelter's communal table. "Are you friends?" I asked, smiling at Aye Mi Mi Kyaw and then at Hla Lay. Beaming, the girls spent the rest of the workshop painting themselves, together, in brightly colored dresses. Each painting included a little house for two.

For adults, life in a refugee camp can be characterized by uncertainty, frustration, monotony and fear. Meanwhile, refugee children, like children everywhere, are curious, playful and bounding with energy. In the confines of a camp, children make friends easily and roam freely. In Isaiah's part of Delhi, the rumble of trucks, mounds of fly-infested garbage along every roadside, harassment, constant threat of muggings and countless other hazards associated with slum life inhibited the outdoor activities of newly arrived refugees. Isaiah's dream was simple. "I dream of playing outside with my friends."

Isaiah (12), New Delhi, India

HOPES & DREAMS

Every refugee yearns for a renewed sense of belonging, reconnecting with loved ones, feeling at home again. After being forced to flee their native land and live in exile in a neighboring country, the 1% of refugees who are resettled abroad often confront homelessness all over again. In the United States, figuring out how to navigate the homeless support system can be profoundly challenging, especially for non-English speakers. However, homeless refugees rarely show up in homeless shelters. Typically more stable refugee families take in those still struggling to find their footing. An aspiring artist, Rah Nay Kaw Htoo felt at home painting his dream home in Karen State.

Rah Nay Kaw Htoo (20), Kent, Washington, United States

Baby Doi (8), Oakland, California, United States; a Chin girl, Aizawl, Mizoram State, India

Lalrindika (19), Aizawl, Mizoram State, India; Moses (11), New Delhi, India

HOPES & DREAMS

Zakir (19), Cox's Bazar, Bangladesh
Photo credit: Steve Gumaer

Roughly 250,000 Rohingya refugees—the vast majority not registered with UNHCR and without access to humanitarian aid—live in Bangladesh. This visual story was painted by Zakir, a Rohingya boy raised in a refugee camp in Bangladesh's southern district of Cox's Bazar. The teenage son of refugees from Burma, Zakir was born in exile. Most children who grow up in a refugee camp only dream of a brighter future. But Zakir believed in the power of his vision and set about developing a plan. One year later, Zakir opened a school in the camp for dozens of Rohingya boys and girls. Today, he is their principal.

"Students deserve to be literate in their own language."

Nattaporn's lifelong dream was to become a teacher. Ethnic Shan, she hoped her students would take pride in their culture. She wanted them to be able to read and write in their ethnic language. In 2014, the Mon State Parliament passed a bill to allow the teaching of the Mon language and culture in government primary schools for the first time in over half a century. All other classes would be taught in Burmese, according to national policy. Students in other ethnic states aren't as fortunate; they must study their native languages on their own time, without state funding. Nationwide, ethnic education departments have continued to push the government for the freedom to teach their ethnic languages. In anticipation, Mon—and Shan—educational leaders have prepared ethnic curricula. "Students deserve to be literate in their own language," Nattaporn said.

Nattaporn (19), Chiang Mai, Thailand

HOPES & DREAMS

Most people in Burma don't have electricity, let alone Internet access. Despite widespread coverage gaps, sluggish connection speeds and steep service costs, mobile Internet access is expected to increase dramatically and become far less expensive in the near future. The government has enacted reforms that promise to improve connectivity for its long-isolated citizens. While in Chiang Mai, Thailand, the young ethnic Kachin man who painted this visual story learned about human rights, rights long denied his people. He returned to Burma eager to introduce ethnic youth in northern Burma to the power of the Internet and their digital rights. "We must advocate for inclusive Internet rights and freedoms."

Anonymous (21), ethnic Kachin, Burma

"We must advocate for inclusive

Kyaw Swa Nyunt, Mae Sot, Thailand

Internet rights and freedoms."

Kyaw Swa Nyunt hosted our workshop in his roadside hut, which doubled as a one-room preschool for children of undocumented migrants from Burma. He dreamed of teaching peace-building in Burma. While most refugees we talked to along the Thai-Burma border dreamed of Burma becoming a federation of autonomous states with rights of self-determination, Kyaw Swa Nyunt, who is Burman, dreamed of a unified Burma. Shortly after our workshop started, I was startled by the arrival of a man in his 30s wearing army fatigues. Kyaw Swa Nyunt introduced the soldier as his brother. Without so much as a nod or a smile, the man took a seat among the children and proceeded to paint his dream of a unified Burma, Burma's official flag. I noticed that Burma's official flag was in Kyaw Swa Nyunt's painting too. A few minutes later, I felt like I had stepped on a landmine when I referred to the children's native land as "Burma." While Kyaw Swa Nyunt fiddled with his watch, his brother barked at me, "Myanmar! Myanmar! Myanmar!"

HOPES & DREAMS

Kyaw Dah Sie (17), Mae Sot, Thailand

Many of the youth who participated in our workshops had been orphaned by an outbreak of violence in their villages in Burma, or were friends of orphans. An orphan herself, Kyaw Dah Sie aspired to graduate from high school, secure a good job and earn enough money to donate to the orphanage that took her and her little sister in when they had nowhere else to go.

"I dream of opening Chin State's first university."

Before departing for Delhi, I scheduled a workshop in Aizawl. Shortly before our family reached the lush, mountainside capitol of Mizoram State, our host—an ethnic Chin human rights activist—had a scare. Local police had learned that one of her workshops had drawn undocumented Chin migrants in Mizoram State as well as Chin who had traveled across the India-Burma border especially for the workshop. While the Chin from Burma scurried back across the border, the local Chin were deported. So instead of running one large workshop, we agreed to facilitate five unassumingly small workshops. Van Lal Thara attended one of our mini-workshops. When asked about his dream, his gaze drifted out the office's east-facing window toward Chin State. After clearing his throat, he said, "I dream of opening Chin State's first university."

Van Lal Thara (27), Aizawl, Mizoram State, India

HOPES & DREAMS

Four ethnic Karen youth in Mae Sot, Thailand

Laom (9), Aizawl, Mizoram State, India

Daydreaming of a brighter future helps refugees of all ages cope with the prolonged uncertainty of living in exile. However momentary, dreaming can offer respite from depression, anxiety, traumatic memories, sometimes even physical pain. Nine-year-old Naom dreamed of being a doctor in Chin State. "I want to help people feel better." As the niece of a Chin human rights activist, Naom grew up knowing that the Chin people needed, above all, affordable health care.

"I want to help people feel better."

HOPES & DREAMS

Iang Te dreamed of returning to her home village in Burma and building a colorfully checkered hospital that would be so warm and inviting that every patient who arrived feeling listless and downtrodden would leave rejuvenated and hopeful. Some of the staff would be like her, former refugees who had been educated and trained while living in exile along the Thai-Burma border. "Even villagers who can't afford to pay will feel welcome."

Iang Te (14), Kent, Washington State, United States

Law River Maung (17), Mae Sot, Thailand

Among the countless medical students who dashed into the streets to aid those wounded during Burma's 8888 Uprising was then 29-year-old Cynthia Maung. Visibly supportive of protestors, she was forced to abandon her studies and flee across the Thai-Burma border. As she trekked through eastern Burma toward the border she encountered ethnic villagers who had never received health care. Moved by their plight, Dr. Cynthia set up a makeshift clinic in Mae Sot, right across the border. Today, Dr. Cynthia's clinic, Mae Tao Clinic, serves over 140,000 patients per year—for free. Most patients have traveled by foot from villages in eastern Burma. In 2012, Dr. Cynthia's name was among those finally removed from the government's blacklist of "enemies of the state." Law River Maung was inspired by Dr. Cynthia's story.

"Even villagers who can't afford to pay will feel welcome."

HOPES & DREAMS

Van Lal Thara (27), Aizawl, Mizoram State, India

Van Lal Thara dreamed of becoming a backpack medic and slipping back across the India-Burma border in search of Chin villagers in need of medical care. Mobile medics serve conflict-ridden ethnic communities throughout Burma. Lugging packs filled with medicine and equipment, they train villagers in health and hygiene and provide lifesaving care to IDPs trapped in densely forested, mountainous and other remote regions. Traveling for several months at a time, backpack medics risk, and in some cases have sacrificed, their lives to serve those in need. While facilitating workshops along the Thai-Burma border in 2011, we met members of the Thai-based Back Pack Health Worker Team. They said nine medics and a midwife had been killed by regime troops or landmines.

"No one wants peace more than us."

Yan Naing Win (18) and Wah Ler Htoo (17), both from Mae Sot, Thailand

Yan Naing Win's life-long dream was to become a professional artist. Yet he felt a moral duty to his people. "First, I will serve in the Karen army." In 1947, independence leader General Aung San—Aung San Suu Kyi's father—signed an agreement with ethnic leaders at the Panglong Conference, promising respect for ethnic rights and power-sharing. Five months later, Aung San was assassinated. As subsequent governments have all reneged on the Panglong Agreement, ethnic communities have been subjected to the ongoing invasion of their land. Wah Ler Htoo was glad that the government had signed ceasefire agreements with most ethnic armies. However, he felt refugee leaders should also be part of ceasefire negotiations. "No one wants peace more than us."

HOPES & DREAMS

Ahimsa, or non-harming, is one of Buddhism's five ethical precepts. To engage in or incite violence motivated by hatred or prejudice goes against the teachings of the Buddha. However, Buddhist extremists claim that, according to their scriptures, violence can be a necessary evil committed out of love or duty. In other words, the (un)acceptability of an action depends upon the perpetrator's intention. Ultra-nationalist Buddhists in Burma have manipulated this belief to rationalize attacks on Muslims as acts of self-defense, in defense of Buddha. Like many Buddhists in Burma, Zin Mar Aung considered violence against any other human being a betrayal of Buddhist values. At the same time, she said that, when 90% of a country's population is Buddhist and Buddhist monks have been the face of the anti-Muslim movement, she wasn't surprised that even Buddhists who practiced *Metta*, loving kindness for all sentient beings, had not spoken out against the violence. "Fear can be a deadly excuse."

Zin Mar Aung (29), Aizawl, Mizoram State, India

"Fear can be a deadly excuse."

Hla Hla Win, Mae Sot, Thailand

With a legacy of early Baptist missionaries, the vast majority of the population of Burma's Chin State is Christian. Hla Hla's father was a pastor. Despite the risks, he delivered regular sermons at a little church local villagers helped him build. One day, soldiers from the Burma Army barged into the church. "They beat him to death," Hla Hla Win said, glassy-eyed. "Then they set the church on fire." Hla Hla Win dreamed of returning to Chin State and fulfilling her father's vision of building a larger church and becoming a pastor, to honor her father's legacy.

HOPES & DREAMS

Hamidi (10), New Delhi, India

Like many residents of the Rohingya encampment in Delhi, Hamidi dreamed of the minaret in her hometown in Arakan State. She dreamed that it hadn't been a casualty of the violent clashes between Buddhists and Muslims in June 2012. She dreamed that former neighbors now living in IDP camps in northern Arakan State could leave the camps and rebuild their homes and communities, safely. She dreamed of reuniting with her Rohingya friends in front of the minaret and of rediscovering how to live peacefully with her Buddhist friends.

Nay Win Aung said that militants at both extremes of the Buddhist-Muslim conflict had exploited deeply rooted fears to promote their respective causes. The conflict dates back to Burma's independence from Britain in 1948, when civil war broke out across the country between the central government and ethnic states. In Arakan State, both Buddhists and Rohinyga Muslims engaged in secessionist movements from Burma. Today, ultra-nationalist Buddhists fear that if they lower their guard, Islam will overtake Buddhism and Muslims will drive Buddhists out of Arakan State and ultimately rule Burma. In an effort to drive out the Rohingya first, Buddhist extremists have branded Rohingya "illegal Bengali." Like millions of ethnic people from Burma who have migrated to neighboring countries, many Muslims have come to Burma in search of better opportunities. However, migration from Bangladesh into Burma's Arakan State goes back centuries. Many Rohingya are just as rooted in Burma, just as worthy of citizenship, as their Buddhist neighbors. Nay Win Aung was realistic. "It's easier to lose trust than to regain trust." A member of an interfaith youth group, he was also determined.

Nay Win Aung (23)

"It's easier to lose trust than to regain trust."

HOPES & DREAMS

A feeling of anonymity is shared by refugees who have fled to a neighboring country. Refugees in Thailand and India often said, "I feel invisible or resented." Inside Burma, ethnic people can feel unseen by the majority Burman population. They have two identities: the one on their national registration card, the other in their heart. The 2014 census—Burma's first census in 30 years—wasn't just an opportunity for greater civic participation. For many ethnic people, it was a chance to assert their true identity and pay homage to their ancestors. The refugee girl who painted this self-portrait had resettled recently in the United States. Only later did I notice that she had painted her face over her name, as if—at least for now, until she felt more accepted—she wanted to be seen but not known.

A Chin girl, Tukwila, Washington, United States

Aung Naing (23), Aizawl, Mizoram State, Burma

Aung Naing arrived alone and sat apart from the other youth in the workshop. I make a point of talking one-on-one—usually through a translator—with each workshop participant. However, Aung Naing never looked up from his drawing. He was so engrossed, I didn't want to interrupt him. Not until after the workshop, after I noticed Aung Naing had left, did I finally see that he had drawn a self-portrait—his dream. In Burma, gay, bisexual and transgender persons have been treated cruelly. Despite progressive reforms, same-sex activity can still be punishable by fines and imprisonment. Each time I look at his visual story I feel sad that I wasn't able to share with Aung Naing how much I admired his bravery.

"I feel invisible or resented."

HOPES & DREAMS

Hea Po (15), Mae Sot, Thailand

Hea Po imagined that in their hearts people around the world have more in common than they could possibly imagine. Hea Po posed the question, "What if we looked like our values?" She smiled, then answered, "There would be less conflict, more peace."

"What if we looked like our values?"

Enrolled in an intensive inter-ethnic English immersion program in Umpiem Mai refugee camp, Kyaw Dah Sie dreamed of establishing Burma's first multi-ethnic soccer league. He believed that if other youth from Burma's diverse ethnic and religious groups had a chance to play and work together, like he and his classmates had over the past year, they too would learn how to live together and appreciate one another.

Kyaw Dah Sie (23), Umpiem Mai refugee camp, Thailand

HOPES & DREAMS

Nyan Thar Myint participated in three visual storytelling workshops.

With the precision and laser focus of an expert draftsman, 13-year-old Nyan Thar Myint was deeply consumed by his creative process. Once he started a painting, he wouldn't come back up for air until he had fully realized his vision. Then he would let out a triumphant sigh. In this visual story, Nyan Thar Myint dreamed of inventing technologies that would promote energy, water and environmental conservation. Initially, other workshop participants—all at least 16 years of age—had little to do with Nyan Thar Myint. Once seen in his element, Nyan Thar Myint suddenly was accepted by his older classmates.

Nyan Thar Myint (13), Mae Sot, Thailand

A Karen girl, Mae Sot, Thailand

The refugee girl behind this visual story wanted to be an environmentalist. She dreamed of teaching people—including foreign investors eyeing Burma's wealth of untapped natural resources—why it was so important to treat our planet like a precious seedling. Looking into her cupped hands, she said, "Earth needs our respect, she deserves our respect."

"Earth needs our respect, she deserves our respect."

HOPES & DREAMS

Brang Nan (20), Kachin State, Burma

Brang Nan had been forced to flee to the China-Burma border due to armed conflict in his hometown in Kachin State. A human rights workshop offered along the Thai-Burma border exposed him to gender issues. For the first time, he questioned why women were rarely seen in photographs of peace talks between the Burmese government and the Kachin Independence Army (KIA). During the workshop Brang Nan concluded that women's perspectives were essential to building peace in Kachin State. Behind the peace dove in his painting are the colors of the Kachin flag imposed on a map of Kachin State. As his visual story illustrates, Brang Nan dreamed of women's voices being heard—and valued.

Aung San Suu Kyi emerged as a national icon during the military regime's crackdown on the 8888 Uprising. In 1991, she was awarded the Nobel Peace Prize for championing democracy and opposing Burma's then military regime. In 2012, Suu Kyi earned a seat in Parliament. Shortly thereafter, she announced her intention to run for president. Despite her iconic status in Burma and abroad, Suu Kyi faces daunting challenges. A clause in the current military-drafted constitution bars anyone whose children have foreign citizenship from becoming president. Suu Kyi's two sons are British nationals. Her efforts to gain the support of the military and (former) generals in Parliament have alienated some of her supporters. Yet Suu Kyi, who has devoted her life to bringing freedom and democracy to Burma, continues to inspire most people in Burma—including young women like Ma Gyi—to work harder to fulfill their dreams and help rebuild their nation.

Ma Gyi (17), Mae La refugee camp, Thailand

HOPES & DREAMS

"Ethnic minorities deserve

For decades, Burma's legal system has operated as an arm of state oppression rather than as an institution dedicated to promoting justice. To restore accountability and end impunity, Burma needs to establish an independent judicial system. Ethnic Chin, Lal Duh Kim's parents—who missed out on an education—encouraged their children to set their sights high. A dedicated student in an ethnically diverse high school, Lal Duh Kim dreamed of graduating at the top of her class, earning a law degree from a top university and becoming a justice in the Superior Court of Burma. She said, "Ethnic people deserve to have a friend in the highest court in the land."

Lal Duh Kim (16), Kent, Washington, United States

to have a friend in the highest court in the land."

Saw Yar Zar (16), Mae Sot, Thailand

Why do so many members of the Burmese government and army believe that upholding their values can only be achieved by oppressing ethnic nationalities? Ethnic Karen, Saw Yar Zar dreamed of a world where impoverished ethnic villagers were considered as worthy of human rights as wealthy city dwellers, a world where their voices rang just as loud and clear. As Aung San Suu Kyi has said, "The struggle for democracy and human rights in Burma is a struggle for life and dignity. It is a struggle that encompasses our political, social and economic aspirations."

EPILOGUE
BRIDGING DIVIDES

BURMA'S DEMOCRACY MOVEMENT HAS REACHED A CROSSROADS, CONFRONTED WITH A CLASH IN PERCEPTIONS OF ITS NATIONAL IDENTITY. A multi-ethnic, multi-religious country, the only way Burma can achieve national reconciliation and sustainable peace is by respecting the rights of all of its people.

However, as Aung San Suu Kyi wrote in *Freedom from Fear*, "Fear of losing power corrupts those who wield it and fear of the scourge of power corrupts those who are subject to it." Today, Burma's government is comprised of genuine reformers, pseudo-reformers and a hard-line faction that has overtly resisted democratic reforms. Afraid of losing their grip on the country, hardliners have stood by as the military has continued to perpetuate human rights abuses in ethnic areas and as ultra-nationalist Buddhists have continued to fan fears of (perceived) threats to Burma's majority religion, fostering a climate of prejudice and impunity.

In 2013, our family traveled to Burma to partner with interethnic/faith youth leaders on visual storytelling workshops. Following a series of violent conflicts between Buddhists and Muslims the previous year, youth had been among the first to organize interethnic/faith initiatives and promote an inclusive peace. At a grassroots level, they modeled how to bridge Burma's deep-seated divides. They illustrated to a society raised on the propaganda of prior military regimes that genuine democracy not only benefits from, but depends upon, diversity.

In our workshops in Rangoon and Mandalay, youth were offered a choice of questions to answer with watercolor pencils and crayons:

> *What commonly divides communities in conflict?*
> *How can trust be nurtured between communities in conflict?*
> *What does "peaceful coexistence" look like to you?*

Visualizing their answers stimulated animated discussions about democratic principles and human rights issues. Aware of our workshops with youth along the borders, they wondered why so few refugees had repatriated—and were pained to hear that democratic reforms had yet to benefit many ethnic areas still under military occupation.

Youth in our workshops in Rangoon and Mandalay hadn't experienced the extreme hardships, trauma or devastating losses of the refugee workshop participants, as illustrated by visual stories earlier in this book. However, until recently they too had only known life under a military junta. Yet their imaginations soared as they searched for new ways to promote peace in Burma based upon empathy, equity and justice—as reflected by the visual stories in this epilogue, painted with *all* of the people of Burma in mind, and heart.

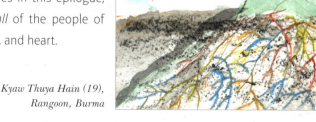

Kyaw Thuya Hain (19),
Rangoon, Burma

EPILOGUE: BRIDGING DIVIDES

Zaw Htet (34), Rangoon, Burma

General Gun Maw of the Kachin Independence Army (KIA) said, "When we are having peace talks with the government, and simultaneously the military invades an IDP camp and treats the IDPs brutally, then it clearly shows that the army is not listening to the government." This issue is rooted in Burma's 2008 Constitution, which reads, "All the armed forces in the Union shall be under the command of the Defense Services." Zaw Htet was skeptical. Until the constitution is amended to hold the Burma Army accountable to the government, how can ethnic armies trust peace agreements with the government? "First, the *military* needs to sign a peace agreement."

Land confiscation by the Burma Army and government has long been a leading cause of conflict in Burma, having displaced hundreds of thousands of people. Conflicts continue to escalate as more and more farmers demand the return of land taken from them for infrastructure, commercial and military development projects. As much of the income generated by these projects has been pocketed by the Burma Army and military-backed conglomerates, protestors are now appealing to the conscience and social responsibility of foreign investors. Nan Hsu Khaing's visual story illustrates the choice facing the military and its cronies: continue to provoke local ethnic armies, degrade the environment and risk losing the world's support—or learn how to respect the rules of a genuine democracy.

Nan Hsu Khaing Thet Wai (20), Rangoon, Burma

"First, the military needs to sign a peace agreement."

EPILOGUE: BRIDGING DIVIDES

Under military rule, Burmans were programmed to believe that federalism equaled disunity and all dissenting voices should be crushed. Before the quasi-civilian government took over in 2011, controlling ethnic regions of the country was the military's job. As the government has loosened its grip, ethnic people have risen up, demanding a truly democratic influence on the political process and decisions that impact their lives. Naing Htet Aung's visual story highlights where the Burma Army has continued to oppress and repress the country's ethnic people. Shaking his head, he said, "The military is greedy." When the army finally learns how to share the country's wealth of natural resources, he added, it will discover that there is plenty to go around.

Naing Htet Aung (19), Rangoon, Burma

"The military is greedy."

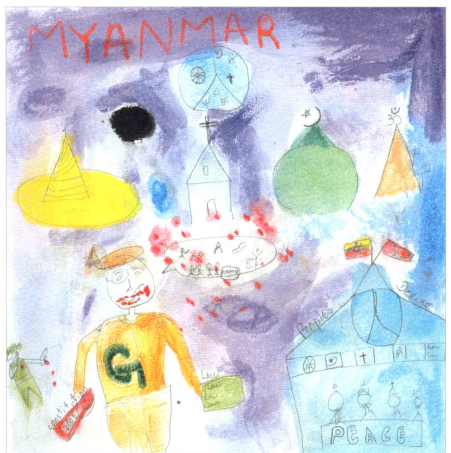

Shine Win (30), Rangoon, Burma

In 1947, General Aung San said, "Only true democracy can work for the real good of the people, real equality of status and opportunity for every one irrespective of class or race or religion or sex … True democracy alone must be our basis if we want to draw up our constitution with the people as the real sovereign and the people's interest as the primary consideration." Less than three months later, he was assassinated and his vision of a democratic constitution, betrayed. In addition to shielding the Burma Army against government control, the 2008 Constitution has institutionalized the "Burmanization" of ethnic and religious minorities, an ultra-nationalistic ideology based on the racial purity of the Burman majority and its Buddhist faith. Until the constitution is amended to engender respect for human rights, equality and justice, Shine Win believed, peace will remain a distant dream.

EPILOGUE: BRIDGING DIVIDES

Wynn Zaw (34), Rangoon, Burma

Raised on ultra-Burman, ultra-Buddhist, ultra-military propaganda during 50 years of military rule, many Burmans confuse racism with patriotism. That includes many Burmese Buddhists who chanted loving kindness for all sentient beings during the 2007 Saffron Revolution. "Ultra-nationalism breeds racism, which breeds conflict," Wynn Zaw said. At the risk of being branded a traitor by ultra-nationalists, a growing number of more moderate Buddhist voices have challenged extremist attitudes and called for a more inclusive society. Unfortunately, they continue to be drowned out by more easily sensationalized ultra-nationalist voices, including those in the government and military.

What is the military's role when faced with ethnic or religious communities in conflict? What are the responsibilities of soldiers? Hlaing Htet Kyaw rejected divide-and-rule tactics: when left unchallenged, fear can spread like a cancer. If he were in command, soldiers would be charged with creating opportunities for communities in conflict to become acquainted, personally. Hlaing Htet Kyaw imagined that when recast as peace builders, soldiers would discover that they could help resolve differences between communities more effectively with a smile and kind words than by forcefully militarizing zones and segregating communities. Hlaing Htet Kyaw also believed that if reconciliation is a genuine goal, the Burma Army, from foot soldiers on up the chain of command, should represent *all* ethnic groups.

Hlaing Htet Kyaw (20), Mandalay, Burma

"Ultra-nationalism breeds racism which breeds conflict."

EPILOGUE: BRIDGING DIVIDES

Burma's transition toward democracy has been viewed from a myriad of perspectives. Idealists say the new quasi-civilian government has implemented democratic reforms in leaps and bounds and that all international sanctions should be lifted. At the other end of the spectrum, cynics say reforms have been superficial and manipulative, designed to distract world leaders and investors from fundamental underlying issues. Sanjay felt that espousing either extreme was counter productive and that extremism merely polarized opinions and entrenched divides. "We are divided by our own thoughts," Sanjay said.

Sanjay (18), Rangoon, Burma

"We are divided by our own thoughts."

Myat Poe Ei San (17), Mandalay, Burma

In Burma, the mixture of religion and ultra-nationalism has been combustible. In 2012, following the first in a series of outbreaks of Buddhist-Muslim violence in Arakan State, Buddhist, Muslim, Christian, Hindu and other religious leaders gathered in Rangoon and established Religions for Peace Myanmar, an initiative that called the faithful back to their shared value of compassion for "the other." Since then, Religions for Peace Myanmar has traveled to areas that have experienced interfaith violence and addressed misconceptions about their respective religions, diffused tensions and promoted interfaith tolerance. Myat Poe Ei San pictured all of the peace-loving people of Burma holding up the country's most vulnerable hearts, regardless of ethnicity, religion or social class.

EPILOGUE: BRIDGING DIVIDES

U Pyin Nyu Jota (30), Mandalay, Burma

Citizens who have been raised within the confines of their ethnic or religious group tend to view issues from a narrow perspective. Isolated from conflicting points of view, they have few opportunities to broaden their mindset. A soft-spoken Burmese Buddhist monk, who was blind in one eye, U Pyin Nyu Jota considered having one's views challenged a prerequisite to becoming a bridge builder. His visual story was inspired by the fable "The Blind Men and the Elephant." In his painting, the four blindfolded men represent Burma's four largest religious groups: Buddhists, Muslims, Christians and Hindus. "We need each other more than we realize."

In a devoutly religious nation like Burma, peace depends upon everyone trying their hardest to look at the world through the eyes of "the other." Founder of an interfaith youth group called Coexist, Htuu Lou Rae encouraged young people to learn about each other's religions. He could envision no better way to allay fears and nurture trust between Buddhist and Muslim youth than by dispelling myths and misconceptions about Buddhism and Islam with greater knowledge of the truth.

Htuu Lou Rae (25), Rangoon, Burma

"We need each other more than we realize."

EPILOGUE: BRIDGING DIVIDES

Active in an interfaith youth group in Rangoon, Aung Kyaw Min Tun had discovered that the best antidote for fear of "the other" is interacting with him/her one-on-one. He considered open-air markets a natural hub of cross-cultural dialogue and cooperation. Markets satisfy a practical need. They are a convenient place to sell and buy products. At the same time, they encourage sellers and buyers who represent different ethnic and religious groups to meet, interact on an informal basis and develop trust and mutual respect, if not become friends.

Aung Kyaw Min Tun (21), Rangoon, Burma

Mitt Tar Hlaing (23), Rangoon, Burma

Experienced with straddling cultures, refugee youth are natural bridge builders. So are youth who challenge their own perceptions by participating in interethnic/faith activities. Whether along the border or in Burma, workshop participants recognized that cross-cultural skills were vital to happiness and success in a multicultural democracy. An increasing number of interethnic/faith youth groups have launched campaigns to challenge hateful rhetoric and promote peaceful coexistence among Burma's diverse ethnic and religious groups. Mitt Tar Hlaing said that participating in an interethnic/faith group had encouraged her to evaluate issues from different points of view. One activity involved visiting different places of worship. "Learning about others' struggles has made me more empathetic," she said.

"Learning about others' struggles has made me more empathetic."

EPILOGUE: BRIDGING DIVIDES

Nang Tin Tin Mya (former political prisoner), Mandalay, Burma

Nang Tin Tin Mya believed every child deserved a quality education. A former political prisoner, she knew that in order to help build a genuinely democratic society, graduates would need what Burma's military regimes had considered a threat: the ability to value human rights, question deeply, participate in policymaking processes and thrive in a country—and a world—where diversity is considered a strength.

Aung San Suu Kyi isn't an exception. Throughout Burma's history, women have proven to be powerful forces for positive social change. Yet, today, women represent only 5% of Burma's lawmakers, and are largely excluded from peace talks. Struck by the relationship between opportunities for women to participate in the political process and their ability to create new opportunities, Mi Thandar said, "Equal rights means equal opportunities."

Mi Thandar Tun (24), Rangoon, Burma

"Equal rights means equal opportunities."

EPILOGUE: BRIDGING DIVIDES

A former political prisoner, influential journalist, human rights activist and founding member, with Aung San Suu Kyi, of the National League for Democracy (NLD), U Win Tin symbolized Burma's irrepressible struggle for democracy. Arrested shortly after the junta's brutal crackdown on the 8888 Uprising, U Win Tin spent 19 years in prison. He was denied medical treatment and tortured repeatedly. Yet his conviction never wavered. "The dictators can only detain our bodies, not our souls," he once said. After being released from prison, U Win Tin continued to wear his blue prison shirt—every day—in solidarity with political prisoners still behind bars. U Win Tin died on 21 April 2014 at the age of 84. Latt Maung Maung's visual story honors U Win Tin's legacy.

Latt Maung Maung, Oakland, California, United States

"The dictators can only detain our bodies, not our souls."

Tun Win Nyein (former political prisoner), Rangoon, Burma

Democracy leader Min Ko Naing described political prisoners who died while in detention as "stars that would never fall from the sky." The government's recent steps toward democracy mustn't overshadow the stories of those who sacrificed their lives and liberty for their country. If it weren't for their irrepressible vision, courage and fierce determination, there would be no quasi-civilian government, no easing of media censorship, no democratic reforms. One day, the truth will surface. Justice will prevail. And the government will begin to repay the nation's debt of gratitude.

EPILOGUE: BRIDGING DIVIDES

Ye Kyaw (19), Rangoon, Burma

Embracing their new found freedoms, youth who participated in our workshops in Rangoon and Mandalay were optimistic about Burma's future. Had I not known that up until two years earlier they had lived under military rule, I never would have guessed. Over the past two years, they had launched campaigns to bridge ethnic and religious divides and equipped themselves with knowledge and skills needed to help build and participate in a democracy. As Ye Kyaw's visual story illustrates, youth in our workshops had discovered the transformative power of grassroots activism.

For half a century the people of Burma were virtually cut off from the international community: 100% of the media was state-owned. Despite an easing of censorship, Burma's media sector still faces the challenge of becoming democratic; that is, also representative of the country's long-excluded ethnic and religious minority voices. And how will those raised on propaganda and rote memorization learn how to differentiate fact from fiction and to engage in respectful debate of controversial issues? On social media, many posts have spread false and biased information, further inflaming inter-ethnic/faith tensions. In 2014, an anti-hate campaign called *Panzagar* ("flower speech") was launched in Burma. On the back of his visual story, Kenneth scribbled, "The fighting peacock of the NLD party in time shall spawn the white dove of universal peace."

Kenneth Wong (46), Oakland, California, United States

"*The fighting peacock ... shall spawn the white dove of universal peace.*"

EPILOGUE: BRIDGING DIVIDES

Thet Su Htwe (30), Rangoon, Burma

Is a truth and reconciliation commission in Burma's future? Government officials, including former military generals, have suggested that survivors of human rights violations in Burma let bygones be bygones. Others believe victims deserve to be heard and perpetrators brought to justice. As the visual stories in this book illustrate, victims of human rights abuses can experience deep trauma. Only if the government is touched by the memories and suffering of survivors will genuine reconciliation—and peace—be possible. Thet Su Htwe said, "Only when everyone is treated with dignity will Myanmar flourish and prosper."

"Only when all of us join hands, can we enjoy this truly

I was intrigued by Aung Chan Nyein Moe's painting of a tea leaf salad or, in Burmese, *laphet thoke* **(pronounced "la-pay toe"),** my favorite dish in Burma. As it turns out, *laphet thoke* was an ancient symbolic peace offering shared by warring kingdoms whenever they had resolved a conflict. Aung Chan Nyein Moe explained that the ingredients needed to prepare this special dish—pickled tea leaves, crunchy beans, toasted sesame seeds, roasted peanuts and soybeans, fried garlic, dried shrimp, chopped kale, cabbage, tomato, cilantro, onions, ginger root, minced chilies and sliced cloves—originate from different regions of the country. In the past, communities could be fundamentally separate, each self-sufficient. With globalization, the actions of one community can impact other communities; the people of Burma have become increasingly interdependent—just like the ingredients in *laphet thoke*. This dish symbolized Aung Chan Nyein Moe's wish for Burma's peaceful coexistence. Smiling, he pointed to the row of figures at the bottom of his visual story and said, "Only when all of us join hands, can we enjoy this truly remarkable dish."

Aung Chan Nyein Moe (19), Mandalay, Burma

remarkable dish."

WAYS TO HELP

THOSE WHO HAVE BEEN MOVED BY THE VISUAL STORIES IN THIS BOOK OFTEN ASK, "HOW CAN I HELP?" This appendix offers suggestions based on my first-hand experiences *on a zero budget*. Resources and web links related to the ideas below, plus more ideas, can be found at the website that supports this book: www.burmavisionsforpeace.org.

BECOME INFORMED

CONNECT ONLINE. If you are a Facebook user, the easiest way to keep pace with the human rights landscape in Burma is to "Like" the Facebook pages of Burma advocacy organizations—for example, US Campaign for Burma—that publicize human rights issues and empower grassroots activists, worldwide, to address those issues collaboratively.

PROMOTE DIVERSITY. For unbiased, issue-oriented news articles about Burma, "Like" "Irrawaddynews" on Facebook. Unlike Burma's state-approved media, *The Irrawaddy* reflects, honors and promotes the country's rich ethnic, religious and political diversity.

EXPLORE WEBSITES. If you aren't into social media, you can sign up for e-news from human rights watchdogs—such as US Campaign for Burma, Burma Partnership, Burma Campaign UK, Network for Human Rights Documentation Burma, Fortify Rights, Human Rights Watch and other organizations listed at www.burmavisionsforpeace.org.

LEARN ABOUT REFUGEES. UNHCR publishes data and reports about refugees, asylum seekers, IDPs and stateless people in/from Burma. The Cultural Orientation Resource Center profiles the history, culture, religion, language, education and resettlement needs of refugees from Burma.

STUDY HUMAN RIGHTS. Before you can help refugees defend their rights, you must know their rights. I recommend watching "The Story of Human Rights" on YouTube and studying the Universal Declaration of Human Rights and the Convention on the Rights of the Child.

BUILD COMMUNITY

JOIN, LOCALLY. If refugees have resettled in your community, you may discover that an informal group of advocates meets regularly to discuss human rights issues in Burma—or you can start one. Networking with like-minded individuals will accelerate your learning curve, inspire collaborative efforts and engage you in global movements.

PARTNER, GLOBALLY. Concerned about specific issues illustrated by visual stories in this book? Identify organizations or advocacy groups focused on those issues. If you support their approach, sign up for their e-news. Publicize their efforts. Ask how you can help. Become a valued ally.

ENGAGE LEGISLATORS. New to the democratic process, refugees can be reluctant to contact their legislators. Offer to schedule a meeting. In my experience, legislators welcome opportunities to meet with leaders of their area's refugee communities. Best of all, refugees discover just how powerful their voices can be, especially when united.

HONOR WORLD REFUGEE DAY. Draft World Refugee Day (June 20) proclamations for your representatives to sign and publicize. Promote a paradigm shift in public perceptions of refugees from dependents of the state to "ambassadors" to developing countries who embody resilience, courage and resourcefulness.

PARTICIPATE IN CULTURAL EVENTS. Ask a local refugee resettlement agency how to be automatically alerted to refugee community cultural events in your area. Open-hearted members of the general public are always welcome. Share your experiences with friends, encourage them to join you—next time.

SHARE THE TRUTH

ASSUME RESPONSIBILITY. Before discovering the power of social media, I rarely questioned the objectivity of what I read or heard on the news. Even though I gravitated toward like-minded reporters, I didn't worry about my perceptions being biased or contributing to divisive politics. Now, I do.

SUSPEND JUDGMENT. Now that I am active on Facebook and my posts about volatile human rights situations reach thousands of "friends," around the world, I am sobered by the responsibility of scrutinizing my sources and investigating perspectives contrary to my own; that is, challenging and refining my judgments before broadcasting them online.

WAGE PEACE, NOT WAR. Before I post a news report or an image to social media, I ask myself: Will it polarize and entrench opinions, or encourage meaningful dialogue and reconciliation? Will it widen divides, or help bridge and heal them? Be on the side of peace.

MAXIMIZE UN DAYS. On Facebook/Twitter/email, use UN-observed international days as "springboards" to increase awareness about under-publicized causes. See www.burmavisionsforpeace.org for a list of international days, including World Refugee Day, International Day of the World's Indigenous Peoples, International Day of Peace and International Day for Tolerance and Human Rights Day.

SUPPORT A CAUSE

VOLUNTEER. If you live in an ethnically diverse community, do a keyword search for "refugee," "volunteer" and your city's name to unearth publicized volunteer opportunities. Also contact local refugee resettlement agencies. Expect to dig deeper for opportunities with refugee-led programs.

DONATE. You needn't have money to donate. You can donate time, helping refugees learn how to navigate the bus system and their new communities. You can donate hand-me-down furniture. Feeling welcome or encouraged can be a pivotal experience for a newly resettled refugee.

PRESENT. Teach others about refugees—why they are forced to flee their native land and how they have inspired you. If you live in an urban area where refugees have resettled, consider co-presenting with refugee community leaders at your local school district office, colleges, places of worship and Rotary Clubs.

HELP A REFUGE SECURE A JOB. Identify employment opportunities. Help develop resumes and cover letters. Conduct mock job interviews. Write letters of recommendation. Offer rides to interviews. For a refugee, no gift is more appreciated than a key to self-sufficiency.

LEARN ABOUT PEACEBUILDING EFFORTS IN BURMA. If you meet refugee youth who would like to promote peace in Burma, share the youth-friendly version of the "Guiding Principles for Young People's Participation in Peacebuilding" at www.burmavoicesforpeace.org.

INITIATE A CAMPAIGN

ORGANIZE A COAT DRIVE. Before being resettled, many refugees have never owned a warm coat, having lived only in warm climates. Each spring, our daughter organized a coat drive at her school. Each spring, her classmates and their parents had a greater understanding of why coats were needed and Seki's donation box filled up faster.

RAISE FUNDS FOR PEACEBUILDING. Encourage friends, family, colleagues—anyone who may be(come) interested in Burma and/or refugees—to buy this book. 100% of the royalties from the sale of *Forced to Flee* will be donated to peacebuilding efforts in Burma. To order, visit www.burmavisionsforpeace.org.

CHAMPION A CROWDFUNDED PROJECT. Search crowdfunding websites for Burma- or refugee-related projects. If you find yourself rooting for one of them, solicit the support of family and friends. If it weren't for our Kickstarter campaign and the generous support it received, *Forced to Flee* never would have been published, let alone accompanied by a dedicated website.

SET UP A SCREENING. Identify a venue for screening a documentary about Burma that draws human rights advocates. Keep in mind filmmakers typically are more eager than their distributors to get their films into the public eye, which is why I contact them directly with a guarantee of media coverage—key to a waived screening fee. Invite a local refugee community leader to speak about issues raised by the film.

CURATE AN EXHIBIT. If you volunteer with refugees, consider how they—given your encouragement—could be empowered to help increase awareness of the challenges and aspirations of refugees. For example, you could invite them to paint what "freedom" looks like to them and exhibit their paintings at a local venue.

FINALLY, DON'T GIVE UP! I have been pained, humbled and inspired by the stories of thousands of refugees. Recalling their stories fortifies my conviction for working on behalf of the inalienable rights we all share: life, liberty and the pursuit of happiness. My hope? At least one story in this book has ignited yours.

THE WORKSHOPS

THE VISUAL STORIES IN THIS BOOK WERE PAINTED BETWEEN 2011 AND 2014 IN WORKSHOPS HOSTED primarily by refugee community leaders along the borders of Burma. Having also been forced to flee their native land, they empathized with the youths' need to participate in the workshops on a volunteer basis and to decide for themselves how much of their lives to share.

Our family's first trip was to the Thai-Burma border. A few days after pulling into the bustling border town of Mae Sot, I met with an art therapist from Ireland who reminded me of the prerequisites of an emotionally supportive workshop environment. Ever since, the responsibility of safeguarding refugees against being re-traumatized by the process of recalling, painting and sharing their stories has guided my efforts on their behalf.

"WE NEED YOUR HELP." That's how I opened each workshop. When I said that the government and democracy leaders in Burma needed to see their stories, stories representing Burma's long-marginalized ethnic people, the youths' brows furrowed. While documenting why they had been forced to flee Burma and what it was like to live in exile, they came to believe my opening statement. No one is better qualified to speak out against human rights abuses than those who have survived them.

While our then 10-year-old daughter Seki distributed the art materials, I would pose questions selected from the questions that organize the chapters in this book. The final choice of questions always depended upon the best interests of the youth, according to the workshop host, in most cases the youths' caretaker or teacher.

At first, many participants were stumped and slightly intimidated by the questions. I would assure them that even those who had never drawn before had painted powerful stories, stories that had inspired viewers to learn more about refugees and campaign for human rights in Burma. I would also clarify that there was no "right" answer, only *their* answer, *their* story. I promised that if they reflected deeply on a question, eventually their imaginations would hatch a visual story—and, as you can see, they did.

As I made my way around the room, a few youth would sit bolt upright, grinning expectantly, eager to share their works-in-progress. Others were too consumed by memories of their past or the creative process to notice me. Still others were engrossed in animated conversation with their peers about human rights issues that had been revealed, at times unexpectedly, by their stories.

Moving from table to table, I would kneel down and quietly acknowledge, assisted by our workshop host-translator, each youth's story, noting and inquiring about a unique narrative element in each painting. If a youth seemed reserved, I would honor his or her boundaries; some youth needed more time to gain confidence in their story and creative process.

Halfway into a workshop, my husband Daniel would ask the youth if they would mind being photographed painting their stories; behind-the-scenes photographs had brought home to viewers the fact that a child created each painting. By now, youth were proud of what they had accomplished. If, for whatever reason, the spotlight made a workshop participant uneasy, Daniel wouldn't photograph him or her.

During each workshop, youth began to believe that their visual stories could help viewers—potential refugee advocates—better understand what it was like to be forced to flee one's homeland and live in exile. They were inspired by the possibility of sharing their stories with the world and helping loved ones they had left behind.

REFLECTING OVER THE 40 PLUS WORKSHOPS I HAVE FACILITATED OVER THE PAST FOUR YEARS CAN BE OVERWHELMING. My memory floods with indelible images of heart-clenching connections I have been blessed to share with youth who wore their fluttering heart on their sleeve, youth who continue to deepen my appreciation of what it means to be a refugee.

Our family has been privileged to bear witness to hundreds of refugee youths' stories. Most inspiring of all has been watching how sharing their stories in a safe and collaborative environment has empowered so many youth to feel a greater sense of control over their lives. Suddenly seeing themselves as catalysts for positive change, they recognize that along with human rights come responsibilities, including the responsibility to challenge injustice and stand up for their rights.

Note: Workshop participants weren't required to sign their paintings; a few of them preferred to remain anonymous. In addition, when I felt a youth's safety might be at risk, I abbreviated or changed his or her name in the credit line for his or her visual story in this book.

If you have been privileged to earn the trust of refugees in your community and would like to offer to help share their stories, feel free to use the "Guidelines for Facilitating Visual Storytelling Workshops" at **www.burmavisionsforpeace.org**.

ACKNOWLEDGEMENTS*

WITHOUT THE SUPPORT OF HUNDREDS OF PEOPLE, THIS BOOK WOULDN'T BE IN YOUR HANDS TODAY. It is impossible to say where my gratitude begins and where it ends when the roots of this ever-expanding, collaborative venture run so deep and the book's fruitfulness will depend largely upon the support of allies I have yet to meet. So I must apologize, in advance, for the incompleteness of the following acknowledgements.

WORKSHOP PARTICIPANTS. First, I need to thank the countless refugee, asylee, migrant and stateless youth who shared some of their most intimate, tightly-held memories and dreams. If only they knew how much their visual stories already have impacted and inspired people, worldwide. They are living proof that even those who have been brutalized and marginalized by society can emerge from the ashes of their traumatic past as a powerful force for truth, justice and reconciliation.

I am also grateful for the young people who participated in our interfaith visual storytelling workshops in Burma, and contributed to the book's epilogue. When violence erupted between Buddhists and Muslims in Arakan State and began to spread across the country, these young people rose up, challenged extremists and then modeled how to build an inclusive peace. Imagine how much refugee and interfaith youth groups could accomplish together, given their shared vision of peace!

I owe yet another debt of gratitude to the more than 70 former political prisoners who participated in a visual storytelling workshop in Mandalay. I believe those who have sacrificed their liberty for the freedom of their country deserve the highest recognition. One day, hopefully sooner than later, Burma's freedom fighters will be honored nationwide, including by the government.

WORKSHOP SUPPORTERS. Of course none of the visual stories in this book would have been painted had it not been for the support of the workshop hosts who welcomed us into their schools, boarding houses, orphanages, monasteries, churches, community centers, shelters and refugee camps. Their names are listed below, by country, and joined by the names of allies who helped connect us. **Thailand:** Nay Myo Aye, Ko Zaw Htun, Lae Lae Nwe, Sarah, Hei Wah, Naw Sunny, Niru Guroong, Phone Myint, Maung Maung Tin, Nyan Soe, Greg Antos, Sandy Shum, Rochelle Ardesher, Niamh DeLoughry, Andrea Jones, Say Naw, Saw Law Plah Min, Aung Myo Min, Derina Johnson, Jen Jones, Hseng Noung and a special shout-out to Garrett

Kostin for facilitating four workshops with Shan and Kachin youth, on my behalf. **India:** Alana Golmei, Dr. Tint Swe, U Dhamma, U Pyinnya Zawta, Kyaw Than, Soe San Dar, U Pannu, Lalsangliana, Pianga, Salai Bawi Lian Mang, Salai Van Hmun Lian, Terah Thantluang, Sawmi Sailo, Van Hmun Lian, Johny Tial Awi, Hla Muan, Lalsangliana Sailo, Van Lai Thian, Zampuii Cenhrany, Syed Mohammad Raghib and Jafar Alam. **Bangladesh:** 19-year-old Zakir, a dedicated Rohingya community leader who, with the help of mutual ally Andrew Day, facilitated a workshop with five Rohingya boys in a refugee camp in Cox's Bazar. **Burma:** Myo Win, Shine Win, Thinzar Shunlei Yi, Htuu Lou Rae Den, Nay Win, Cham Tha, Moe Thu Kha, Ashin Gambira, U Adicca Adicca, Ashin Sopaka, U Aggadhamma, U Zawana, Ashin Issariya, Ashin Javana, Khon Ja, Mary Tawm, Iris Sao Siri Rupa, Kyaw Moe Tha and Nyi Nyi Aung. **United States:** Simon Khin, Pwint Htun, Ta Say, Juliet Ningpi, Jennifer Quigley, Myra Dahgaypaw, Htun Aung Gyaw, U Pyinya Zawta, San San Maw, Jeanne Marie Hallacy, Htun Htun Gin Gyi, Steve Dun, Mona Han, Gloria Grimm, Gary Hallemeier, Nwe Oo, Kenneth Wong, Nyunt Than, Susan Hayward, Nay San Oo, Edward Lee Vargas, Clair Chean and Elizabeth Norville. **Canada:** Zipporah Devadas and Lisa Sadler.

BOOK TEAM. A labor of love, this book project was propelled by a small yet dedicated team that supported the book's development from beginning to end, before (paid) work and into the wee hours. Graphic artist extraordinaire, Alexandra Rösch, transformed my barrage of text, visual stories and photographs into a striking design that, as you can see, honors the youths' life stories. She also designed the dynamic website that extends the benefits of the book and introduced me to her filmmaker husband, Florian Zeitz, who created the video for our Kickstarter fundraising campaign. For those consumed by a project, as I have been by this project since 2011, objective scrutiny is vital. My eagle-eyed copy editor friends Stephanie Lawyer and Garrett Kostin poured over numerous rounds of pages, until they were squeaky clean.

Despite their demanding schedules, the following ethnic community leaders, organizational directors, artist-activists, journalists, authors and educators reviewed the book pages and offered corrections, suggestions and heart-felt testimonials: Aela Callan, Therese Caouette, Laurie Dawson, Larry Dohrs, Beth Farmer, Rachel Fleming, Paul Fuller, Alana Golmei, Oddny Gumaer, Margaret Hinson, Pwint Htun, Khon Ja, Andrea Jones, Saw Kapi, Khin Ohmar, Tun Khin, Naw K'Nyaw Paw, Chris Lewa, Nai Aue Mon, May Ng Wai Wai Nu, Tin Tin Nyo, Patrick Pierce, Margot Pires, Jamal Rahman, Anna Roberts, Benedict Rogers, Alan Senauke, Matthew Smith, Emanuel Stoakes, Voravit Suwanvanichkij, Larn Tai, Hayso Thako, Chaw Ei Thein, Sally Thompson, Jack Dunford, Phil Thornton, Feraya Ullathorne, Francis Wade, Matthew Walton, Kenneth Wong and Sonya Wyrobek. Each and every page of the book benefited from their knowledge, first-hand experiences along the borders of Burma and diverse ethnic, religious and political perspectives.

CLOSEST TO HOME. I was raised by a father who wrote dozens of letters to newspaper editors challenging our country's decision to go to war in Iraq, despite receiving death threats … at the age of 82. He instilled in me a fierce sense of justice and a belief in my ability to mobilize support for a just cause. You were right, Dad. Just look above. I was also raised by a mother who immigrated to the U.S. shortly after World War II, when being half-German and half-Japanese meant you were a former enemy. When landlords in San Francisco refused to rent an apartment to her, or years later—I recall, as a child—passersby spat racial slurs at her, she continued to hold her head high, determined not to let them derive the satisfaction of knowing that she was crying a river of tears inside. I owe my allegiance to those treated unjustly to you, Mom.

Above all, and with heart in hand, I am grateful to my husband Daniel and daughter Seki Thu. Besides agreeing to spend our limited vacation time and dwindling savings the past three years volunteering along the Thai-Burma border (2011), along the India-Burma border and in Delhi (2012) and in Burma (2013), they were integral to *Forced to Flee's* development. In addition to taking most of the photographs in this book, Daniel has been my #1 champion. Even when I was spending more money on the project than I managed to secure in grants, he continued to believe in the book's potential and my ability to see it through, offering feedback and encouragement each step of the way. I will need the rest of our lives together to prove just how grateful I am for the sacrifices you have made, D.

FINALLY, I GET TO TELL YOU ABOUT SEKI, whom I adopted as a three-month-old baby, eight years before she introduced me to Daniel. When I taught English to newly resettled Vietnamese refugees in Seattle, Seki—starting at the age of two—repeated after me, right alongside "our" students. Seki was four when we traveled to the remote mountain town of McLeod Ganj, India, to organize art projects with refugee children who had fled Tibet over the Himalayas. When it was time to say goodbye, she didn't want to leave. 27 September 2007, Seki, then six, was swaying on my lap in front of the computer when we happened upon a video of thousands of Buddhist monks streaming through the streets of Rangoon. Leaning into the computer screen, our eyes widened. Despite knowing nothing about Burma, at the time, we were riveted. The next weekend, Seki clutched our hand-painted "BURMA NEEDS YOU" placard at a rally in downtown Seattle. Ever since, my beloved muse has been by my side, encouraging refugee youth to share their stories. Seki, may you one day discover your own swift current and the never-ending gift that you are.

* Throughout this book, the names of many of the visual storytellers were changed or abbreviated to protect their security. For the same reason, I excluded from the Acknowledgments the names of some of the workshop supporters and reviewers of the book.

A Personal Note

As the daughter of an immigrant who experienced the horrors of war first-hand, I was taught at a young age that no matter how rocky my life could be in the United States, compared to children forced to flee war, persecution and extreme poverty in their conflict-ridden native lands, my life was–and would always be–one of privilege.

On the Fourth of July 2006, my then five-year-old daughter Seki was among the dozen "Children of the World" in Seattle's 22nd Annual Naturalization Ceremony. Dressed proudly in her native Vietnamese "ao dai," Seki and the other foreign-born children paraded up onto the stage and proceeded to lead the audience –480 newly sworn in U.S. citizens–in the Pledge of Allegiance.

Later that night, I lay wide-eyed in bed. The final stanza of the pledge–"Liberty and justice for all"– replayed in my head while shadowy scenes from stories shared by my ESL students flashed across the ceiling. After recalling one too many stories of injustice, I typed the e-mail that would change the course of my and Seki's lives forever. With a final deep breath, I resigned from my 24-year publishing career.

I had no idea where the current that I–and my brave little girl, clutching my hand–had leapt into would take us. Only that it was swift; in my experience, a sign of rightness … Listening to refugees share the stories behind their paintings, witnessing their inner voices become emboldened by their own visions, has been the most awe-inspiring aspect of my privilege, facilitating visual storytelling workshops in exiled communities.

I will never forget returning from our trip to the Thai-Burma border in 2011. Tucked under the seat in front of me were all of our workshop participants' paintings, my only carry-on luggage. I gulped audibly at the overwhelming responsibility of having been entrusted with their stories–597 fluttering heartbeats–and of finding each of them an ever-expanding audience of potential supporters.

My wish? That the youths' visual stories haven't just moved you. Instead, they have gripped your heart and will compel you to do–and keep doing–whatever you can to help fulfill the youths' visions of a more just, inclusive and peaceful Burma.